Advance Praise for The Nar

D1124964

"Intelligent and intimate, fierce and tender, real and raw, Paul Lisicky's *The Narrow Door* is an unforgettable memoir about love and loss, friendship and forgiveness. It had me in its thrall from page one."

—Cheryl Strayed, author of *Wild*

"Paul Lisicky's *The Narrow Door* circumnavigates the often inscrutable forces that bring us in and out of each other's lives and hearts, while paying welcome homage to the oft-unsung role of friendship in them. While Lisicky bears witness to 'the hell of wanting [that] has no cure,' his ship always feels buoyant, by virtue of a narrator whose attentiveness to feelings both big and small is marked throughout by honesty and devotion."   —Maggie Nelson, author of *The Argonauts*

"Relentlessly self-revealing, achingly tender in the way he holds his loved ones and the world, Paul Lisicky has written a memoir as raw as Jeff Tweedy fresh from rehab, and just like a Wilco album, packed with tracks, so elegant in their bewilderment and sorrow, you'll want to visit them again and again. This book charmed me, moved me, upended me, indicted me, compelled me, wrecked me, made me want to say the big YES, made me want to be better than I am."

—Pam Houston, author of *Contents May Have Shifted*

"A beautiful, funny, devastating book about love, friendship, and loss that manages to be simultaneously timeless and keenly attuned to our precarious moment. Few things I've read so perfectly capture both the communion and the competitiveness of writers' friendships. *The Narrow Door* is a miracle of personal narrative, observation, and feeling."   —Peter Trachtenberg, author of *Another Insane Devotion*

THE NARROW DOOR

Also by Paul Lisicky

Lawnboy
Famous Builder
The Burning House
Unbuilt Projects

THE NARROW DOOR

A Memoir of Friendship

Paul Lisicky

GRAYWOLF PRESS

Copyright © 2016 by Paul Lisicky

Excerpt from "The Kitchen Table: An Honest Orgy" © 2007 by Denise Gess. Reprinted with permission. Originally appeared in the *Sun*.

Parts of this book originally appeared in the *Boiler, Clockwatch Review, Ecotone, NANO Fiction, Sliver of Stone, Sweet* (reprinted in *Philadelphia Stories*), *Wag's Revue*, and *Yalobusha Review*.

This publication is made possible, in part, by the voters of Minnesota through a Minnesota State Arts Board Operating Support grant, thanks to a legislative appropriation from the arts and cultural heritage fund, and through a grant from the Wells Fargo Foundation Minnesota. Significant support has also been provided by Target, the McKnight Foundation, the Amazon Literary Partnership, and other generous contributions from foundations, corporations, and individuals. To these organizations and individuals we offer our heartfelt thanks.

Published by Graywolf Press
250 Third Avenue North, Suite 600
Minneapolis, Minnesota 55401

All rights reserved.

www.graywolfpress.org

Published in the United States of America

ISBN 978-1-55597-728-3

2 4 6 8 9 7 5 3 1
First Graywolf Printing, 2016

Library of Congress Control Number: 2015952176

Cover design: Kapo Ng

Cover photograph: Feilo Poon

He rested there a little while to recover from the effort involved and then set himself to the task of turning the key in the lock with his mouth.

—Franz Kafka, *The Metamorphosis*

Contents

THE NARROW DOOR

Part I

Volcano

2008 | Our feet are warm. Our faces shine. The room is getting dark, the night coming a little sooner these days. Should I turn on a lamp? Then the prospect of dinner changes our placement toward that dark. The chicken stew on the trivet. The moist leaves in the hard black bowl. The macaroni and cheese still bubbling, although it's long been out of the oven. For a moment, we're no longer eight years into the new century, in Philadelphia, in a loft apartment that's too big for us, but inside a cave, a tight, sweet space. We give our joints and muscles over to the heat of it, the spell, the hearth at the center of things. Our gestures say, we're here for you, time. We're all right with you. We're not straining against your grasp. No concerns about the side effects of the latest round of chemo earlier in the day. No cheering on the small miracle of the meal, the first meal she's cooked since July's diagnosis. No anxieties about the election, the results of which will crackle across the country, throughout the world. No steroids, no PET scans, no CAT scans, no ports, no hoods, no wigs, no hair coming out in wads—none of it. We are the four points of the clock: her mother at three, her sister at six, me at nine, Denise at midnight. See how we hold that clock in place? Nothing but us now, one breath, one body in the room. This table, this bread, forks lifting again and again to our mouths.

But in the world of our Denise, stillness is death. If illness weren't ragging her brain, she'd be driving to Chester County later tonight, to the apartment of the lunatic golfer with whom she's had the best sex. Or she'd be steaming through Fairmount Park on in-line skates, or laughing with a friend, or arguing with that same friend—any opportunity to slam up against the unexpected.

Abruptness, collision, anything to wrench her awake. As if she needs to be wrenched awake. For God's sake, she has more electricity in her than the train yard on the other side of the river. The freight cars bang tonight, startling us, with all the suddenness of thunder. Or is that really thunder, a storm coming toward us from the west side of the city?

She gets up from the table. She walks to the kitchen, brings back a second loaf of bread, sits down. She looks happy tonight. She props up her chin, looks at us with a satisfied gaze with melancholy in it. Still, it cannot be so easy to see the two sides in her—the writing side, the family side—embodied in the group of people she loves, sitting across the table in peace. Complete peace: they're not supposed to live in peace! How would she get any writing done if all she had were peace, no mother to say, can't you write another story? I don't know about this one: Where is happiness? Must everything end that way? Of course all Denise wants is peace, because she never gets any. There's always someone to call on her, need her, in the middle of the night. Think: animals scrabbling the bark of a tree. Does she ever get to sleep?

The flames shudder on the candlesticks. The TV harangues from the living room. We're talking about the election again, our terror, the disaster of the past eight years. The relief is that we're all on the same side. We couldn't have sat together if we weren't on the same side—at least on this night. Imagine the strained politeness of the conversation, the frozen hole at the center of our talk.

Somewhere, I imagine, maybe in Bucks County, maybe just two floors above our heads, a white man sits in front of the TV. He twists the bath towel in his hands. He can't give his mind over to the fact that the black man might win. If the black man does win, this man will rise up tonight. He'll walk down the street. He'll push another black man who's coming toward him with a bottle in his hands. (*Just like a black man to be coming down the street with a bottle. Jesus Christ. Wipe that smile off your face,* he'll say, trying to knock him off his feet.) While two streets away two college students will throw open their windows. They'll bang pots and pans, cry up at the stars, no sense that there's anything but joy in the world tonight.

Some of their joy is filling up the apartment right now. It's not pleasure or delight but tougher than that, more encompassing, more dire. Is it just the news, the stirred-up molecules in the air? Or is it still the hearth of us, the memory of those twenty minutes on the couch earlier today? Her mother and her sister not yet in from Mullica Hill and Mount Laurel, and Denise needing to rest up for the night. "Could I put my feet up on your lap?" she said. "Well, sure," I said, shyer than I expected. She swung her head to the armrest. A book in my hand, her legs over my legs: how light the weight of her. She went right under, the sounds of her breathing calming the room. Funny that it took us twenty-six years and cancer to get here. Ease with each other's body. It doesn't matter anymore that she's straight and I'm not. See how we've been a little bit in love all this time, and not able to say it? But that's the story of any friendship that lasts this long. All those hours on the phone, in restaurants, in classrooms, or at the dog park—you couldn't do all that and not be in a little bit of love.

Now she looks at the bookshelves, the paintings on the walls. Maybe it no longer seems like the place she had to settle for after giving up the apartment of her dreams. Two weeks in that apartment— two weeks! All because it was three flights up, stairs, stairs, and more stairs. And what of that day she had to sit on the second landing, weeping, waiting for someone to carry her to the third floor because she didn't have the energy? Nothing was worse than that. At least she has her elevator now. Life on a single floor, with a decent washer and dryer, just in case she shits those new, expensive jeans. Her family is here; I am here. So what if her hair comes in puffy, white, and dry, if the chemo's clouded her magnificent eyes, if her cat's gotten radiation sickness from curling up on her still-taut stomach? She lifts her chin. She starts dancing. Not a timid dancing, but a life-large, goofy, it's-great-to-be-in-my-skin dancing.

"Stop," her mother begs, as if it hurts for her to watch it. "Stop! Please! Denise!"

But her mother should know better than that. Denise only dances harder.

2010 | *Eruption.* I look up the word and assemble as many definitions as I can find. There's a strange comfort that comes from making a list, a collection. Eruption as disease. Eruption as outburst in a crowd, on a street. Eruption as volcano. Every day in the world a volcano goes up. Just today, January 5, two volcanoes have erupted: the first in eastern Democratic Republic of the Congo; the other, Turrialba, in Costa Rica. Both mountains are far from towns and coffee plantations and are thus of little interest to the news machine.

But the volcano that snags my attention is Mount St. Helens, the first volcano to go off in a major population zone in an industrialized country. I put off writing some more by wasting time on YouTube, mesmerized by footage of the 1980 explosion. The footage isn't actual; it's built of still images in the manner of an old-fashioned cartoon. What startles me is the clarity of the lava. The lava slides down the mountainside in a silvery wash, with the translucence of saliva, pre-come, tears. It takes down a side of the mountain with it. It takes down birches, buildings, cabins. It buries tractors, mailboxes, mule deer, though you can't see any of that from here. I refuse to say the earth is reflecting my feelings; the story of perception is more complicated than that. But the earth is certainly having some trouble with itself, and I keep playing the video over and over, until I feel both better and a little sick about it.

I scroll through the comments on YouTube, all of which are written with the calm precision of people who know what they're talking about. It's a wonder that these comments still appear with regular frequency, as if the mountain went off just two years ago, not thirty, and the people are still hearing the grit on their windshields, spitting ashes from their mouths.

—*I was finishing at Detroit Lake when at about 8:30 I heard a sound that closely resembled heavy naval ordnance at sea. I had no idea Mt. St. Helens let go at that time. This might have been a distance close to two hundred miles.*

—*I was a little kid in Victoria when this volcano erupted. Crazy. It sounded like thunder with too much sharpness. Then later the ash.*

A few clicks later, a photographer's website:

—*As the smoke rose in the sky, the wind picked up. Specks of pumice were lifted like sandpaper grit, smashing into the few obstacles on the surface sparse landscape. There was little chance to escape the constant bombardment.*

—*Spirit Lake was inundated with fallen trees and volcanic debris. The fallen forest still floats on the surface of the lake.*

I look up from my computer and two hours have passed. What about the book I'm trying to write, the book that wants to bring back my friend?

I scrawl a little math on the back of an envelope. Today Denise has been gone four months, two weeks.

Her eyes: playful, wry, soulful.

Her charisma, her wattage. A movie star.

Her old plea, the old accusation, "Nobody loves me." Or worse: "You don't love me." And her joy when I shut my eyes, or gave her that look that said, I've had all I can take of you.

Her quickness to laugh, the laugh that came from deep in the body. Part silly, part womanly.

Her cup of scalding-hot coffee, held with both hands, close to the collarbone and throat, even if it was ninety-seven degrees outside.

Her toned olive arms.

Her monkey feet.

Her ability to walk into any room and warm the atmosphere. A ray of energy moving right into you.

2008 | It's the third afternoon of the summer writers conference. I've loosened up enough to admit that I dislike the room they've given M and me. There's no sunlight, and for several hours every afternoon, the family next door turns on the TV as the kids run in and out through the orange trees out back, shrieking. It feels transgressive to say, I don't like this place, I don't like this muggy, dark room, as this gig is especially prestigious. I might be violating some pact between us about making the best of our lot. Am I complaining? A look of confusion registers in M's blue eyes before it's gone.

M yawns and stretches, sitting up from his nap. M is a poet, six years older than I am. We've been in each other's life for seventeen years now, four as friends, thirteen as lovers. For years I've traveled with him to readings and conferences, where every so often I'm asked to read and teach, too. It's not always easy to be away from home so much, to be open and friendly to strangers when you're feeling tired and shy and not terribly strong, but I love this life. I'm so much inside my life with M that it's hard for me to see it, name it. As much as I pretend to, I don't even mind the psychic challenge of it—this morning it was the administrator who laughed derisively at my name as she admitted to misspelling it on a poster. It is enough to be with M, really. To watch him reading a book, his brow intent, enmeshed in thought, beautiful thought. Clear eyes moving from left margin to right. A smile breaking light into his face. I am safe, fully myself in his presence, and that's not anything I've ever felt into my blood before.

In a little bit, all nine members of the faculty will meet at the drive-in, a much-loved place in town that hasn't been renovated since the 1960s. Picnic tables, burgers, french fries in paper boats, grass, flowers, and those remarkable California bluebirds flying from tree to tree to tree.

But before I change into my shorts, I check my email. Among the three new messages, an unexpected name.

> *Denise Gess asked me to write to you. Last week Denise was taken to the hospital she is at Penn Presbyterian at 39th & Market. I'm very sorry to tell you, she has been diagnosed with cancer, she is in room 565 the room's phone is not connected Denise is using her cell phone.*
> *Doris Granito*

My heart should be beating, but it is not beating.

I try to take in the palms outside the window, but they blur. The lawn, absurdly trimmed, hosts the brother and sister next door. They run before our windows, throwing a mottled orange at each other's back.

I read the message again. I tell M. I lie down for a minute, talk to M again. He rubs his eyes; he's still a little foggy, still waking up from his nap. I read it one more time, get up, put on my shorts.

I believe it will help to brush my teeth. I squeeze toothpaste onto the brush, but more of it ends up on my hands and sleeve than on the bristles. I glance up at my face in the mirror. If the news were serious, I'd have heard from Denise's brother, her sister, her daughter, Austen, by now. Doris Granito? Denise can't stand Doris Granito, the woman who lives down the hall from her, the woman who tries to act like her, dress like her, talk like her, only to get it all wrong. The woman with the same initials, who believes this is a sure sign that they're sisters, lovers.

Toothpaste bubbles at the corners of my mouth.

Doesn't Doris know Denise? Denise is a burning torch, Denise is a firestorm. Denise has already beaten cancer, colon cancer, six years ago. Cancer is a fucking joke in the face of Denise.

I take another look at the email. I shake my head at her delivery, which seems simultaneously cranked up and dead. In days Denise and I will probably be rolling our eyes and sighing about the tone of this note. Poor Doris, we'll say; her whole life has been streaming toward this moment. Anything to be at the center. But that's the thing about Denise. The people she's hardest on are the people she thinks about the most. And maybe that's why people like Doris throng to Denise. For who else but Denise ever looked to Doris with such light in her face?

A half hour later I'm laughing with the others at the picnic table. The night is sweet, windless. There's a smell of lawn clippings and wet mulch. It astonishes me that I can turn off the disaster and listen to my friends. Claudia and Nick are discussing bewilderment as an aesthetic, what it might mean to how poems get made. They're having a hard time of it: how *does* one talk about the ineffable? In another life I would have used this window to talk about *my* bewilderment, the news that came to me an hour ago, and my worry would have been the subject of our night. But not tonight. We need this night. We need to pass Nick and Lili's baby back and forth, not just for the weight of her—feel her between your hands, lighter than a bag of sugar—but for the wonder of looking into another face. Isn't that why people lean toward babies and dogs, after all? We want to look into a face that isn't going to judge, dismiss, or hurt us, but one that looks back at us with amusement, a face that makes us wide awake.

Maeve moves from one set of hands to the next. She smiles, reaching toward us with a hand no wider than two of my fingertips together. She squeezes my fingers hard, as if to say, Look! Beware! Maeve is strong!

Across the country Denise tries to be perfectly still as the technician pulls the hood down over her eyes.

Rehearsal

2008 | *Finally, some quiet time in which to write you. Darling,
I heard your messages and love them so much, but usually when I get them it's before a procedure, after one
or in the middle of something. Sorry I have not spoken
with you yet.*

*Okay. Here is where we're at presently. Take a
breath . . .*

*Not only is the non-small-cell cancer in the lung, but
it invaded the fluid in the pericardial sac, so while the
fluid is gone now, my heart has cancer as do the lymph
nodes along the trachea and a few in the neck. We got
the uber bad news on Monday that the MRI showed
the cancer has metastasized to my brain. There are
17 lesions, mostly in the cortex; two teeny tiny lesions
but scarily a shade too close for my comfort near the
cerebellum. Long story short—this development altered
everything in terms of the order of treatment. We must
get to the brain first and everything else after.*

*Yesterday they called me in to meet the radiology
oncologist. I love him. He's excellent. And today they
brought me in for a PET scan and mask-making mold
of my face. Very freaky which I will wear when they
begin radiation on Monday. They are doing whole brain
radiation, five days a week, for three weeks in fraction-
ated doses. I will feel deeply fatigued and will by the
ninth day lose all my hair. When radiation is done, then
it's on to chemo which will be more uncomfortable.*

    Tomorrow I go again, wear the mask, then they map all the markers for radiation. I must lie completely still for one hour.

    So today, I came home, made an appt. and had my hair cut short. I figured it would be less painful to part with short wads of hair than to see my long hair fall out. Also I figure it's a way to embrace a new head rather than resist what I cannot control.

2010 | Six months after Denise's death, M and I are standing before a four-foot-wide nineteenth-century photograph of a crowd on the beach. We're in Cape May, at Congress Hall, the old hotel with the forty-foot pillars, where the picture in question hangs in a low-lit hallway. It's almost impossible to make out any details. Maybe that's because the photograph itself is showing its age. Some might call the color of the paper sepia, coffee, soil. To me, it is the color of Time, though I don't want Time to be that color. I don't want it to cloud or grime or seep into everything. Right now I want it to be clearer, brighter. If it can't be a color, then it should be the white of the snow around the shrubs outside.

    And yet, what is worse than a room where there's nothing old, where the chairs and paintings have been bought from the same furniture store at the same time? No signs of fading, chipping, loose threads, or paw prints. Or the water stains on this photograph, from which we can't quite tear ourselves away. There's a shipwreck, a lighthouse, and two bird sanctuaries down Sunset Boulevard, yet here we are, on a cold January afternoon, sinking into the nineteenth century.

    How often do we get to see this many people at once, fixed? I think people are beautiful when they're together like this, even though I know I'm not seeing them as individuals. From here I can't see their resentments. I can't see them wounding the people they care about or jockeying for position against one another. This is a production. It's likely the hotel had put up a sign by the front desk: GET YOUR PICTURE TAKEN BY THE PIER AT NOON! The people on the beach seem to know they are part of a larger scheme (advertisement?), so it's no surprise they do what they can to resist it. One stands with a foot in the surf, looking toward shore. One hands another a baseball or a piece of fruit. Another drapes his arms over the shoulders of two muscular men, as if to claim them as brothers. Off in the distance there's a lifeboat—or maybe that's just the dark head of a swimmer— the lifeguard inside trying to protect bathers from going out too far. These people must have money. Their casual indifference suggests they don't need any more attention than they're getting. There is no lack in them. But it must be work to pretend it's a casual occasion. And in that way they have no idea how fragile they look.

I wonder if they know they might be rehearsing for their deaths. Probably they were asked to hold still. Thirty seconds, thirty minutes. Maybe a whole afternoon went by when they could have been moving around in their good clothes, getting ready to go out for fried chicken or oysters. Very likely it wasn't a single shot. Keeping still is harder work than digging a ditch. Why would they even put up with this, on a sunny day in summer, if they didn't want someone 122 years later to do exactly what we're doing: standing in a hall on a wintry day, asking who might that have been? If their souls could see what we're doing, wherever they are, whatever they are, would they be saying, Watch me? Pick me?

I glance over at M. His eyes are as clear as they've ever been. Is he imagining W, his late partner, into that crowd? I imagine he is, blue eyes following W out into the waves as if W has lost all semblance of human form and become a marine creature. W has been gone for sixteen years, but M's attachment to that fact does not shift or diminish. Death shadows his face. It draws him away from me. I have willed myself not to feel apart from M when he goes to this place. I have learned not to think: *replacement—I am not his great love.* The love coming at me is the love intended for the lost. I'm swimming in it. I'm trying to ride the wave of it. And yet I have been chosen. I have *enjoyed* being chosen, picked out from the crowd.

I place my hand on the small of his back just as a hotel bartender hurries through the hall, smelling of fireplace.

Maybe now that Denise is gone, I'll have a better sense of what it is to be M. Maybe that will make us closer.

Imitation Jane Bowles

1983 | "Paul?"

I sit up in my desk chair as if I've been shocked awake. I'm in my little office on campus, where I've been reading and marking up five-page process analysis essays. This particular essay—thirty-eight of fifty—details the steps involved in blow-drying your hair, and though the writer thinks the sound of her voice is funny, it isn't funny at all. I've been circling on the second paragraph for the past twenty minutes. I'm not so far off from drooling, with one eye crossed.

Denise waves some papers in the air. Her earrings quiver. Her face gleams as if she's just coming down from teaching a wonderful class. She is a second-year teaching assistant at Rutgers; I'm just starting out. Unlike me, she's able to hold the attention of an entire group of freshmen. They listen to her, rapt, as she tells funny stories about the comma splice and fused sentence, while I must work very hard to control my stage fright in order not to throw up all over some girl in the front row.

"Let us make love like a couple of crazy angels," she says. And breaks out in a deep laugh as if that line were the funniest line ever written.

The line is from the story in her hands. The story in her hands is mine, one she'd asked to see last week.

She says the line loud enough for everyone in the English department to hear. Dr. S, the Shakespeare professor, with the natty blazer and the lockjawed vowels, hears it; Phyllis, the department secretary, part my aunt Vicki, part Chita Rivera, hears it, too. They go on typing whatever it is they're typing, but there's no way they're not leaning in, listening, because these halls are small, and let's face it, we all need distraction from the wonders of process analysis.

Denise pulls up a chair beside me. If only I could be present enough to take in that gaze, to stop sensing obligation in it, my life would change in an instant. I'd no longer be a lowly graduate student, but be like her, a writer whose first novel is poised to make a splash. I'm still mired in my past, a past that says, she likes this story more than it deserves to be liked. Yes, I've worked on every word, chosen every description with the greatest care, but the story still sounds like imitation Jane Bowles—which is exactly what it is. Yes, the characters might have some life in them, but the best of them fall out of the story, never to be heard from again. Things happen without foreshadowing. I'm pretending to mock and shatter narrative, to make fun of story convention, but the truth is that I have no control over what the hell I'm doing. I should tell her the story is meant to be nothing more than a cartoon. And as far as the seriousness that's expected of literature? I don't yet know how to be serious. The only thing I know how to be is silly, to make people laugh, which is why I've written a story about a fifty-five-year-old spinster who meets a thug on the street who fucks her silly until she wakes up parched, cross-eyed, and wigless, with her head at the foot of the bed.

Denise sits so close, I can feel the heat off her. There's a scent about her, the faintest perfume, a little cigarette, black coffee—sex? She must be surprised that I don't lean back into her. She's probably used to people pushing back into her, as if they're playing games with their bodies. I'm all packed up inside myself like a house that hasn't been opened in years. And when she does touch me to underscore a point, I tense. I wonder if she feels me springing shut. When anyone touches me, it feels like it's an electric shock, and I won't find my body again.

Her voice shifts, her shoulders draw back, her voice gets quieter, more neutral. She's reached into a different room in herself. She's restrained now, teacherly. She is drawing from the place that makes her students listen. "Now here she wouldn't say that," she says, pointing to some dialogue on page three. She's not talking about me, or herself, but she's talking about writing now. She herself is part of writing now, as I am part of writing; she's teaching me how to detach, to respect the story's wishes as distinct from my own. She is teaching me not to be bewildered, defensive.

But soon enough she's back to laughing about the things she likes about the story. Control, though necessary to our project, is only bearable for so long. We're back to silliness and the real reason I wrote the story: to make somebody laugh. We're laughing harder; I'm letting go of my wariness, and we're probably on our way to flooding the English department with disruption and delight, all the feelings that aren't usually expressed here. Phyllis shifts in her rolling chair; Dr. S clears his throat with a gruff, exaggerated sound that expects us to make use of its command to shut up. His throat clearing suggests that we're not worthy of the task at hand—we don't know the least of it when it comes to the discipline required of literary study. If only he knew that control was already written in our blood. People like us—Catholic school kids, children of social aspirants, grandchildren of immigrants from southern and eastern Europe—have already been spanked and shushed into submission. The real work—though we're not able to see it yet—requires us to throw off those old coats of obedience. The coats have been on us so long we don't even know we're wearing them. We've been tricked into thinking they're light and beautiful when there's only lead in their threads.

Or perhaps Dr. S is just jealous he isn't one of us right now. It must be irresistible, if a little lonely, to be so close to the sound of two people fast becoming friends.

A World Out There

1946 | Roberta Joan Anderson looks out the window of her house at the train tracks in Alberta. Snow on snow, the layers so deep, no one can even say how much has fallen by January. The snow doesn't go anywhere; her parents don't go anywhere. Sometimes the snow doesn't let them leave the house, and if they do leave for a concert or a movie, it requires wrapping themselves in multiple scarves and layers and gloves. Why would her father, just back from the war, want to go anywhere? Former flight sergeant: he has seen enough brutality, enough of the world. It is definitely before Roberta has polio. It is definitely before she starts smoking, at eleven. It is definitely before she's known as the singer Joni Mitchell, or given up a baby girl, Kelly Dale, for adoption. She looks and looks out the window, as if by sheer looking she can transform the landscape. The train that she waits for every night—she hears it first, an ominous but satisfying rumbling; then a sweep of light, lunar blue, as if the moon has turned up its wattage—roars by with the transformative power of an explosion. It cuts through the snow like a knife. It says Canada is just a place to be passed through, and for that moment there isn't just a bed and a window frame, but a *world out there.* And the world inside—her father with his trumpet and his Harry James records, her mother with her school prep and mops—recedes. The train says that the world they're in is not as big as she thought; these lives are as weightless as the flakes her friend shakes into her goldfish tank.

Thirteen years after those winter nights, Denise stares out the bedroom window of a split-level on a cul-de-sac called Catalina Court, in Somerdale, New Jersey. She can't take her eyes off the backyard at the house beside hers. Mad Dog is on a tear and nothing in this world is safe. Mad Dog is the name she's given the woman next door, the mother who's always fretting, always lashing out at her kids, whose infractions are nothing more than the usual kid kind: talking too loudly, stepping on new grass, leaving handprints on the foyer walls. Today Mad Dog has put her oldest son in a dress and has ordered him to march around in circles while she watches from the back step. The boy marches around the perimeter of the backyard with a calm, neutral face. The boy will not cry. The boy will not let his mother get what she wants. In an hour he'll get this over with, and he'll sit down and do his math homework, and maybe she'll even reach into the freezer and give him a cherry Popsicle, his favorite. She won't even mind if the red drips down his fingers onto his sleeve, where it will stain the fabric for good.

Does Mad Dog know that a girl is watching her through the second-floor window frame? If so, would she make Denise come down to watch with her? Or would she put her in boy's clothes? Denise does not feel any urge to call Joey, her brother. She knows if she does, he'll start laughing, and she'll probably start laughing with him. Maybe later they'd even bring up the story within earshot of Bobby. Maybe they'd even imitate his march in front of him: a boy putting on a girl's hat—the teasing kids will do! Soon enough Bobby would be the laughingstock of the cul-de-sac, that paved bulb of a street where the neighborhood kids play kickball and tag. Denise wants to keep him her secret, she wants to live inside his pocket, where it's warm and sweaty and a little sad. She steps round and round the backyard of her own imagination, engraving a shape that won't ever let her rest.

2009 | No one is walking the halls of the bathhouse tonight. The floors are clean, the ceiling is clean. My sheets, towel, and pillowcases are clean, which should lift my spirit, but I can only think about Denise, with whom I've spent the better part of the day. She's in her last hours. It's early Friday night. Anyone who would be here is already off to Rehoboth Beach, Fire Island, New Hope, or Asbury Park, any of the gay weekend resorts within driving distance of Philadelphia. But

I couldn't bear the intensity anymore, all those faces turned toward Denise, waiting for her to go. She wouldn't let go.

My stare is vacant, deliberately vacant. I am performing it. I am perfecting it. Music thumps the speakers, music that's working too hard to express transformation and joy. That is okay. I'm too stunned to feel, anyway. My mind is still inside that hospice room, the Joni songs, the nimbus of warmth and confusion surrounding that bed. Maybe that's why I'm here. I thought I'd wanted to touch someone. I thought I'd wanted to escape myself, but maybe I want just the opposite: a cool dark space, tight walls, low ceiling, where I can be attuned to the sound of my breathing again.

Denise would understand. She'd have asked me all about it, would want to know the details, eyes wide open and in awe. She'd have said "why couldn't I be a gay man?" with mock exasperation. But she'd have meant it, too, without any of the self-delight or condescension of people who often say such things.

A skinny young guy with burning eyes hurries down the hall. He backs up, stops at the door of my little room, with an affable, devilish smile. He seems interested. I might be interested, too, but he keeps on walking. Not with the aura of rejection, but because it's better to keep moving than to stake your claims on any one person. I think it's incredible that such places stay open, what with Grindr or Scruff or any of the other smartphone apps. Why keep them open? There has to be some better reason than simply to extend the last hours of an old tradition, which barely exists anymore.

Then another man, thicker, more muscular, appears at the door. My response is instantaneous, animal. My spine goes straighter. The other face is hard, squarish, a smart head shorn to the scalp. All bone and plane and brow. Salt-and-pepper whiskers. A salt-and-pepper pelt on chest and shoulders. In his eyes, certainty, solidity, gravitas. On the street, in a different neighborhood, he might be thought to be a construction worker who spends more time than usual shaping and trimming his beard. But in here I know better.

Skin against skin, salt and musk and heat of mouth on mouth, on chest, stomach: whose body is whose? I shouldn't be able to answer that; I should be so immersed in my skin that the remix on the sound system doesn't matter. The fact is that I do know where I begin and end. I'm looking at myself from myself. A stance is wanted from me—a male presence, a take-chargeness—though I can't find the part of myself that could give someone else those things. At least not now.

All those faces looking at Denise. The thunderstorm outside, the candles in their cups inside. "It's All Over Now, Baby Blue" playing in the room. I don't know why this song, of all songs, made me pause and well up when I first heard Joni's cover of it. At the time I thought she was only singing about herself, the end of youth, the artist who was identified with *Blue*. But it's not just that.

All your seasick sailors, they are rowing home

And joy? Well, whatever it is, joy feels elsewhere tonight. Not in this city, not in this palace of empty rooms.

The man sees questions on my face. Somehow he knows how to sit back and let me say, *my friend is dying*. He asks questions about my friend and I tell him everything I'm able to tell. I'm careful not to use up his patience, as I know how easy it would be to do such a thing. He's a nurse, he says, and knows a thing or two about burying people he cares about. And it doesn't matter if we end up screwing each other senseless or not. It doesn't matter if the chemistry isn't right for tonight and I can't stay hard for him. Kindness has happened instead. He puts his arms around me from behind. Then plants a dry kiss on the back of my neck.

And, piece by piece, he hands me back my clothes.

Later, though M will be touched by this story, I'll wish that he had wanted me to be home with him tonight.

Dig

1984 | Two in the morning. A twenty-minute walk from Pine Street to the nearest station of the PATCO train, which I must take in order to get back home to my parents' house across the river in Cherry Hill. The prospect of taking that walk, of waiting for the train, and going through all the rituals that need to be done before I climb into my bed, the twin bed of my childhood, keeps me pinned to the couch. Besides, it's never easy to tear myself away from Denise. I never want to walk away, even though she talks too much, even though she often doesn't let me get a word in. I love the slouchy white chair, the Picasso print of a hand clutching flowers, the low humming light of the lamps on the table—how the hell does she ever see? Beyond the bathroom door, I see the impeccable bedroom, where the deep-blue spread is pulled tight across the mattress, the pillows propped up against the white headboard, fresh yellow tulips on the nightstand. It is clearly the most important room in the house, waiting for its next guest. It is far from the safety of my family home, and I like that about it. I'm deep inside the realm of adult drama, of romance and betrayal and fucking: life transpiring in front of me.

Now Denise is walking back and forth across the living room. She is holding her cup of coffee between two hands. She puts it down, lights up a cigarette, inhales from the cigarette, reaches for the cup of coffee again. She is talking about her former teacher, Famous Writer, the writer who writes big, fat, funny-sad novels with violent accidents in them. She has corresponded with him for years. He has written to her; she has a stack of his letters to her in which he'd given her every reason to think that his marriage, a marriage to a woman he still loves, is over. Nothing could be so wrong about ripping each other's clothes off, as she puts it, and spending the night together.

"Why doesn't he love me?" she laughs, in a voice that knows it's the dumbest question ever asked.

She holds up the cover of the issue of *Time* on which he appears in a red T-shirt under a tan blazer. His face looks tired, gruff, unshaven, hurt, horny. It's the face of someone who thinks his suffering is more meaningful than yours. I like his books, especially the one in which the son loses his eye on the stick shift, but I'm troubled by his hold on her. It might be the case that Denise wants to *be* him more than she wants to be with him, but I believe she'll figure that out in due time.

I wish she'd stop. I wish she'd talk again about *Franny and Zooey* or *Good Deeds* or the professors and TAs and any of the other grad students we know in common. Instead, she's filling up the space with Famous Writer—or more precisely, Famous Writing. She is going on for hours with it. My eyes are grainy, my tongue thick with listening to her. And yet there's a high buzz of excitement in the air. Outside, on the sidewalk, is Philadelphia—hear the four Archbishop Wood students cursing at some drunken girl across the street? But inside? We are characters in an Almodóvar film yet to be made. Coffee makes sluicing sounds inside the coffee maker. A cigarette burns in the ashtray socket. Joni's *Wild Things Run Fast* is playing on her cassette deck. And now we're sitting together on the sofa at 1 a.m. on a Saturday night, waiting for the damn kitchen phone to ring.

Just like that, it does ring.

Denise leaps. She looks at me, lets the phone ring one more time before she picks it up. And as a hello comes out of her mouth, a dial tone.

"See?"

We stay in our respective positions until the process repeats itself all over again. Another hang-up, then another.

"You think it's him?" I say, a little wary.

"Of course it's him," she says, her smile getting bigger, her voice half thrilled, half hurt. Does she show me a log? I picture it on a legal pad, marked with the exact times of the hang-ups, as well as the number of rings and the length of seconds before the connection clicks off.

"He's afraid. Men like him—*men*," she says, drawing out the word, frowning at me.

"Always afraid. Cowards." She picks up her cup again and puts it down a little too hard on the tabletop. A little coffee slops over the rim. "What's wrong with men? What's wrong? *You*."

"What?"

"Man. *Man*—"

"Me?" My collar feels tighter around my neck.

"Pauly," she says, her voice softening, her features softening, going pretty again. "Do you think I should go up there?"

By "up there," she means the writers conference in Vermont where she was his student, where he's teaching right now. I should just tell her that I'm out of my league, that, though I'm twenty-three, the mechanics of heterosexual romance are as comprehensible to me as the compounds that make up sodium chloride. I'd know more about building the Golden Gate Bridge than I would about men and women and the games they play regarding sex.

Her face shines. She keeps looking at me hopefully, expectantly, as if I might pull the answer from deep within myself, if only I listened.

But she's weeping now. The weeping isn't merely about Famous Writer and her wish to be with him, to be him. Or the hell of competition. No, her tears seem to be about the hell of wanting, which finds its way underneath your eyelids and fingernails and has no cure. I don't know why I don't get up from the sofa and put my arms around her. I don't know why I sit with my hands practically folded on my lap, hoping she'll shake herself out of it and start talking about J. D. Salinger again. She is on the left side of the room. I am on the right.

We might as well be on different sides of the country, yet I could be the one to change all that. I could cross that charged space. I could close it up with my body, and the crying, the awful crying, would stop for the night.

I should just say it. I should stop keeping that starved landscape inside myself a secret. Men are on my mind all the time, not that I ever do anything about it. Certainly that must be evident in how I move and talk and walk through a room. And it's not as if she'd be anything but all right with it. Her student John came out to her in her office one day, after an exasperating class discussion when it was assumed that men wanted one thing, and women wanted the opposite, and that was the problem from the get-go. *Well, I'm not any of those people,* John said, and Denise loved him all the more for his stubbornness, his red hair, his stark, charismatic ferocity. In fact, she brings up John all the time. But to say that I'm a John would be to say that I'm not the person she thought I was. The person she holds in high esteem. The person she thinks of as a promising writer. The person she thinks of as handsome, though I don't know what the hell she means. I'd just be one thing, a gay thing, the person who creeps into the adult bookstore on Route 73, slips quarter after quarter into a slot (all the quarters he saves for this purpose), and dreams into the images of a forbidden world he both desperately wants to be a part of and is desperately afraid of. A world that couldn't feel farther from the pine trees and strip malls and new subdivisions along Route 73.

There must be a good reason I keep my grandeur to myself, but I don't know it yet. It is a little like a secret animal, with oily rank whiskers, I don't want Denise to know about.

Can Denise already see I'll be with another Famous Writer in eleven years? Can she already see how happy I'll be, in a life she'll only be a guest in? The menagerie of animals, M and I reading our first drafts to each other, roses outside, the fireplace burning . . .

Maybe it hurts to sense that coming. She's already beginning to spell out an equation: Paul is the lucky one. Paul gets everything I don't get.

"Should I go up there?" she says once more, the road map of Vermont unfolded across her lap.

I look at the length of that route, up the spine along the Hudson, across mountains, down steep grades, roads that turn and twist through villages. I think of her worn-out Buick, the car that struggles up the slope of the Ben Franklin Bridge. "Yes," I say. "Yes." Even if I guess that's not what she wants to hear from me right now.

2010 | Darlene Etienne is pulled from the rubble in Port-au-Prince after fifteen days. It's hard to picture it: fifteen days under the rubble of your apartment. You're living on nothing but the little bit of the Coca-Cola you ration daily for yourself. You're still calling out for help, even though you sense your rescuer isn't anywhere near. You're just doing it to move your throat membranes, because it feels better to move them than to keep them still. That movement keeps them from hurting, drying up from the dust. Then a relief worker from France hears you calling, but barely. He sees a puff of your black hair when you're probably minutes from your own death, and he starts digging. Digging and digging and digging, with such noise and activity and a plea for you to hold on (is he digging you up, or is he digging himself up?) that you've forgotten how thirsty you are, how your tongue feels like a wood chip in your mouth, how your skin hurts when anything rubs against it. And not much later, you're part of a story that's not even about you any longer, but the absurd spectacle of reporters, relief workers, and your fellow citizens cheering and applauding your dusty body as it is hauled into the back of an ambulance.

And as for J. D. Salinger, who dies today?

I'm in the middle of writing the previous paragraph—I've distracted myself by looking at Twitter—when the news comes in. It takes a good twenty seconds to hit, and when it does, I stop writing. My attention isn't capable of much, even as I wonder whether my reaction is authentic. Perhaps I am enjoying the private theater of it all—luckily I'm all alone in the house today. Maybe my body just needs to weep. Maybe I haven't even wept since Denise's death. I have become a little hard these days, my bullshit detector extra-refined, scalpel-sharp. I'm wary of any writing that wants to provoke tears, any gesture that has the slightest stink of familiarity about it. Anything that asks the reader to say yes to some received truth.

So what is it I'm doing? Why do I step aside from my story to start digging up quotes from Salinger's work? As soon as I find them, I post them, and watch in wonder as people comment and pass them around:

> Maybe there's a trapdoor under my chair, and I'll just
> disappear.   —*Franny and Zooey*

> Life is a gift horse in my opinion.   —*Teddy*

> Seymour once said to me—in a crosstown bus, of all
> places—that all legitimate religious study *must* lead
> to unlearning the differences, the illusory differences,
> between boys and girls, animals and stones, day and
> night, heat and cold.   —*Franny and Zooey*

The depths these quotes sound. Brashness and tenderness and crankiness and love. Self-absorption and loneliness, the loneliness of the unheard, the unseen. The cadence of plain speech, expressive and overwhelmed, overstimulated. A voice that's been so absorbed into American literature that you can't even hear it as distinct anymore. How far that voice seems from the cool, neutral tone of minimalism. A week or so later I'll pick up the *New Yorker* and read

Adam Gopnik's tribute and find two quotes that will seem to say everything—at least for that moment:

> The message of his writing . . . [was] that, amid
> the malice and falseness of social life, redemption
> rises from clear speech and childlike enchantment.
>
> It was the comedy, the overt soulfulness, the high-
> hearted (to use an adjective he liked) romantic open-
> ness of the early Salinger stories that came as such a
> revelation.

The other revelation, the visceral revelation bringing about those tears, is that those stories fed us once: Denise, me, Famous Writer. All the way from the tone and characters to the constellation of names. Our work spoke back to that work: it paid it homage. How could we have forgotten that? Maybe it is just that Salinger was the voice of youth, and it was inevitable that we'd outgrow that voice as our interests turned toward the work of adulthood.

But my guess is that there's another explanation. A voice goes out of fashion. A voice gets associated with popularity, which translates to pandering. It is said that Salinger loves his characters too much, and we say, yes, you might be right. He can't possibly see that you might not want to put up with a seven-year-old Seymour going on and on and on. He simply isn't generous enough with his audience. And as for the difference between imagination and reality? Well, he should have a better handle on that.

And someone dies and everything comes back to you. You think: That voice fed me once. That cadence is in my writing, my speech, my hearing. In what I call my ear.

I go back to the sentences about unlearning the differences. I get two cranky replies to my posts from people who think Salinger is mediocrity incarnate, the end of standards. *You tell me how you can "unlearn," Professor,* says one. And I take some pleasure in telling the young man that it must be a lucky thing to know so much.

Unlearn. I don't go back to see the passage in context, but I do feel its purity, its faith in the breaking down of boundaries, the good of that. The quote is the kind of quote Whitman would have liked. The narrator is talking about the act of making, the act of refreshing the world for the weary traveler who thinks he's seen it all. And the most amazing thing is that these words are received on a crosstown bus, which dissolves the line between east side and west.

How could we have forgotten him?

Or the young woman, for that matter. That young Haitian woman is found six days after the rescue mission had called it quits. Of course they'd called it quits. The prospect of finding anyone at this late stage, in horrible condition, is too much to bear. Better to declare everyone dead and make it official. Better to kill hope and go on with the next thing.

Then I remember the obvious truth: it is all too easy to let go of the things we loved once.

1984 | Denise is outside the Barn at the Famous Writers Conference arguing with Famous Writer. The day is windy, dry, bright—or mostly bright. Clouds tower over the mountain. These aren't summer clouds; they look like winter. They anticipate the first frost, which will come sooner here than any other parts of the Northeast. Who knows what Denise and Famous Writer are saying? Other writers—teachers, staff, students—walk by, pretending to look away. Later, they'll probably talk about it at dinner. Later, they'll compare notes: Do you know anything about that woman? Yes, she was a contributor here; she wrote a novel that's coming out in the spring. But their real interest will be Famous Writer, whose gruff face has lost any tinge of its smoky handsomeness this minute. He is older. His hands are flying up, just as Denise's are flying up. They make chopping motions to underscore a point. He's lost any air of patrician boarding school control, and it infuriates him—this is happening before his colleagues, his students. As quietly as possible, he says, *I can't see you now, I don't want to see you. I think you might be crazy.* And he storms off inside the Barn, to leave Denise standing outside.

Does she look out toward the buildings, the kelly-green shutters, the butter-colored clapboard? Does she look around for someone who might know and support her, another contributor from last year? Does she hold herself with her arms, or does she let those arms hang free, waiting for Famous Writer to walk out of the Barn to say, I'm sorry. Maybe her heart is beating too fast for her to register it. Maybe she simply walks out to the highway, looks to her brother, who's waiting in the car beneath a tree, studying sheet music on his lap. *Go,* she says. *What happened?* Joey says. *Let's go,* she says, louder now. *Den,* he says, and shakes his head. *We've driven all the way up here. What did that jerk say to you?* But she motions forward with her hands, remains silent, as if the whole thing is Joey's fault, and they're off, past the general store, past the creek rushing along the roadside, through the woods, down the mountain into town.

Already the director of the Famous Writers Conference might be making sure Denise is never asked back. At least that's the way she'll tell it to me for years.

The same argument, transmuted, is central to her second novel. An entire book travels toward that confrontation, but there are no emphatic hands, no passersby. The scene doesn't take place in New England, but in a Manhattan apartment, in a different Famous Writer's apartment. The two lovers—or lovers who never were—don't even yell. Their feelings are too big for yelling; language can't contain even them. Indirection, withholding, silence, pause: all of that hurts more. But Emily, the central character, will not be humiliated, will not be a victim to her own wanting. The exchange, as devastating as it is, brings about satisfaction and peace. Not instantaneously, but in a little while, after the death of Emily's mother in a bus accident. The important thing is this: A boundary is drawn. Fame is on the left side of the room, the Manhattan side of the room. And she is here.

And life might just be possible after that.

2009 | My devotion is dog-like, I know it. I like looking at the tops of M's ears, which stick out fetchingly from the sides of his head. Blue transparent eyes, trimmed whiskers around the strong and subtle mouth. But it's his cerebral side that captivates my attention. Remoteness, austerity, mystery—I catch myself fixing on him, for minutes at a time, from the Eames chair across the living room. I wonder, what, what gears are turning inside his head? What are his plans? I only take my eyes off him when he catches me looking.

And yet, more often than not, there's been some powerful exchange of psychic materials between us. M and I catch ourselves putting on the same style of jeans at the same time—one of us must change; we don't want to be *that* kind of couple. We have the same perceptions at the same time. I bring up Michael and Luis just as M professes to think about Michael and Luis. How has their renovation been going in Hell's Kitchen? It's been unnerving, profound, though we laugh about it, this connection. No wonder strangers are always wondering whether we're twins. If we wanted to, we could wear each other's clothes.

Animal

1967 | A thick breeze blows off Newport Bay; the breeze smells of seaweed and salt and boat engine. It cools the arms and necks of the throng in front of the stage, but not enough. Joni Mitchell is down among the crowd. She still feels good about the set she just played, but the day hasn't been the best. Judy Collins, who was supposed to pick her up at her building on West Sixteenth, called her up from the festival to say, I'm already here. Competition once again: isn't Judy the one who sells all the records? So Joni had to find another way to get there, and walked up to the stage, still out of breath, just minutes after her arrival.

She eases through the throng with Elliot Roberts, her manager, at her side. Some people smile at her; she half-smiles back. The people are careful to give her some space, and besides, their eyes are turned to the new act on stage. She is looking to find the bathroom, or at least some water to drink. It has been so long since she's had anything to drink. Her throat is grainy, muddy. The air temperature is actually rising minute by minute, and there's no space between bodies. It is beautiful to be down here with the people—she knows that—but it is all a little much.

Are you Joni Mitchell? says a young woman.

The girl's voice is sweet; it couldn't be further from unkind. Her face is innocent, if there could be such a thing as innocent. It's the kind of face she'd want to sit down and meet if she were anywhere else. But its intensity strikes silence into Joni's nerves. The need in her has nothing to do with Joni. The face doesn't exactly want to devour her—it's nothing as extreme as all that. But there's pressure in it. The face says, *everything you do is significant; every gesture of yours will be recorded, interpreted, remembered, copied.* Her face says, *you are living out my life for me, but you're doing it better, with more poise and beauty than I ever could.*

And how does Joni react?

She turns in the other direction. She runs like a deer until she is far, far outside the gates of the festival.

1976 | Maybe Joni can also see that wanting in the face of the young woman who somehow gets close to the stage at Philadelphia's Spectrum. Maybe there's just a flash of that face before the spotlights turn on and blind her. Persistent girl, stubborn girl. Those girls are always around, down in the orchestra, climbing up the towers toward the lights, wherever she performs. She has to think past that face if she's going to get through "Coyote" and "Don Juan's Reckless Daughter." All everyone wants to hear are early, simpler songs that make them cry, that conjure up the lost nights of their youth, in dorm rooms or in boyfriends' beds.

Denise watches Joni from the black zone, through chain link. Joni is wearing a short jacket, a red bolero. Her eyes look exhausted, but she is investing every line, vowel, and break with personality. She is not phoning it in, even though she could certainly be doing so at this point in the tour. The speaker in "Coyote" thinks of herself as a hitcher, "a prisoner of the white lines on the freeway." There are lovers to be met along the road, on ranches, in roadhouses. She watches a farmhouse burn down, the domestic life going up in flames around her. She loves these men awhile, then heads back to the highway once she realizes the life of the artist is not about routine or staying put. It is a bold new persona for a female pop singer, a role that inverts the usual gender convention. The woman is in power, the man left behind at home, stunned, wounded, hurt. "Why'd you have to get so drunk / And lead me on that way?" says the coyote. The audience goes crazy with applause. They can't get enough of these songs, that persona. For Denise, Joni is longing perfected.

1984 | The upper room of the bar is low-lit, with amber sconces on the wall. It hums with people. Denise's family is there; her editors are there, people from the Philadelphia press are there. Members of the English department and fellow graduate students. At her side is Sam, the lawyer in tortoiseshell, horn-rim glasses, who seems to have modeled himself on a Bryn Mawr WASP; his most distinguishing characteristic is that he's scrubbed himself of particularity. I shake his hand, say hello. He says hello back. Since they started dating a few months back, he has been prone to saying things such as: *I like you more than I like your book.* Or: *I like you but I don't love you.* Denise has run these statements by me just to see whether she's not being oversensitive. My role is to exclaim, *he said that to you?* Maybe Sam knows Denise has already run such statements by me, which would explain why he's all too eager to be led away by Denise to her editor.

In the center of the room is a white cake. It is a *Good Deeds* cake, a facsimile of the book cover designed by Fred Marcellino. There's a drawing of the ladder on the cake, with stylized, elongated arms reaching upward on the rungs.

Toasts are made. To the success of the book! To the success of the next book, and more and more and more books until there's a great tower of books, a great tower of Denise. Denise says a few words; the publisher, who's come down from New York, says a few words. Then a man with a knife cuts the cake with all the finesse of a brain surgeon.

I have not moved from my position by the stairs for an hour. I talk with my fellow teaching assistants; I make small talk (why does small talk make my throat tense?) with people whose names and connections I can't make out above the din. Then a woman is standing in front of me, so close to me that she's made sure a conversation is required of me. She is as imposing as an Alp. She is as deafening as a waterfall. Part Wicked Stepmother, part East Berlin barmaid, part Sandra Bernhard. How old is she? Large nose, very large eyes and chin. And beautiful, in her own particularized way. I'll call her Wyatt here.

I have no idea what Denise and Wyatt have in common.

According to Denise, Wyatt lives within view of the Philadelphia Art Museum, in a high-rise apartment building where she is one of the few residents who isn't a Jewish senior citizen. She, along with her father and brother, are the people the characters in *Good Deeds* are modeled on, though Wyatt seems nothing like the no-nonsense, sensible narrator who tries to save her screwed-up family.

I tell Wyatt that it is good to meet her—finally.

Wyatt tells me that she's heard nothing but good things about me. "I have to see this Paul person Denise is always talking about. She just won't stop. All I hear these days is Paul did this and Paul did that. It's getting tiresome!"

We hug. She kisses me. Everything we say after that comes with a smile, the kind of smile that suggests all of our words are a joke.

She asks if we're going to spend some time together soon.

I say, of course.

She says, "This weekend?"

I can feel the apprehension playing out on my face. I think, I can't possibly spend time with you this weekend.

The more she looks at me, the more I want to be anywhere but in this room. I want to be in my twin bed in my quiet house on my quiet street across the river, where I can think about the party and review it in my mind, without having to feel any of the queasiness that comes from actually having to talk to a person, especially a person with a bigger personality than mine. There is a large vibrating mouth around Wyatt that seems to suck down everything that comes near her. If I could step back from myself and see the intricate, sensitive person inside her, I could see that Wyatt is probably as scared of this party as I am. Is she afraid of losing Denise? Is she going to lose her best friend to editors, agents, people who want to make money off her, all sorts of hangers-on? Those are things I've been too afraid to consider, and maybe that's why she's come over to me. She sees the wanting in my eyes. I'm the only person in the room whose needs might be greater than hers.

She asks if I have eaten any of the cake. There's a lurid quality to her pronunciation of *cake*, which involves a twisting of the upper lip, with the slightest grimace. But there's a generous quality to it, too, which is strange.

I shake my head back and forth, but smile. I always smile, especially when I'm with someone who bewilders me. If you put me face-to-face with someone pointing a gun at me, I bet I'd still smile, even today.

"You should. Try some. Ready?" She offers a piece of cake. The piece I take is slightly too big to fit; I can't get it all in my mouth without getting frosting on my lips, so Wyatt asks the woman standing next to her for a napkin, and with the damp napkin she wipes off my face.

I glance over to Denise. She is talking to a very good-looking, sharp-featured man. His important face seems to brighten, as if promises and little deals are being passed back and forth. But Denise's face is the more serious of the two. From here it has some drama in it, like the face of someone confessing turned to a priest.

If only I could keep up with Wyatt! Her banter demands that I be as showy as she is; she doesn't leave room for sincerity. My shyness makes me so self-conscious, so fucking *boring*, and I loathe myself for it. *I'm not the person you think I am,* I want to cry out to her, but maybe she already knows that and there's pleasure, of an almost scientific sort, in watching me trying to catch the ball then throw back the ball. I am a dog—yes, that's what this feels like—but not a dog who's been around a long time, not a dog who knows the rules of the run or the park, but the skinless runt of the litter who hasn't even been neutered.

Then it occurs to me: is she trying to find out about me, the life I'd rather keep hidden?

"Excuse me for a minute," I say. "I'll be back in a minute."

She says go ahead, as her eyes turn to the man in the pink bow tie.

On the way to the restroom, I run into a professor from the English department whose eyes look off to the side. His mouth is tense. It isn't Wyatt's mouth; there isn't a grimace in it, but it's lonelier, less certain, as if he can already see ahead to difficult times.

Does he see in my face what I see in his? Do we come to the same realization at once? Oh, yes. Denise is leaving us.

2009 | The upper room of Culver City's Museum of Jurassic Technology is low-lit, with candles in glass votives beneath a painting. The painting is a portrait of Laika, the Soviet dog, the first dog in space. There is an absurdity about the sentimentalized rendering, the aura of reverence in the room, especially in a museum that wants to test our relationship to what is being seen, interpreted, displayed. Are we being played with again? M and I don't know. But even if we are being tested, we're only further disoriented by this invitation to feel. Here, we've learned to wonder but to hold our wonder ten feet away. And now we're just unnerved. We don't know who we are, or what a museum is supposed to do.

Is it too much, then, to imagine Laika's last day on earth? It is plain fact that Laika never came back—we all know that, no one knew how to get her down. Let's just say that Laika's last day was her best day. Say that she wasn't to be swabbed with alcohol and fixed with wires. Say she wasn't to be subjected to tests of sound and heat and what it felt like to be weightless for hours on end. Instead, we will say she's thinking of her time at Dr. Lavel's house. Dr. Lavel, who gave her a cedar bed, and let her sleep at the foot of his own wide bed. Who cooked chicken especially for her, seasoned with marjoram, thyme, and rosemary. The smells of that house so familiar that she'd almost forgotten she'd ever been a street dog, sidling up be-side street people to keep warm. And her diet, as if it could ever be called such a thing: pencils and garbage and lead.

On the day of the Sputnik launch we will say Laika was met by a parade. Say President Khrushchev held her high above the crowd, and the crowd clapped and cheered and blew red plastic horns, scaring the crows away for miles. Say the people in that crowd knew they were meeting a hero, whose work would lead to sense and peace, and never to one more war. Decide that she was able to take in this praise, believe this praise was for her alone. As for her panting? Say it had nothing to do with stress, and if there was stress in the moment, it transformed her instantly into light.

Decide that the capsule she was trapped in was comfortable, gave her room to walk around. Decide that she was touched on the face before they closed the door. That the rocket launcher wasn't too loud, the temperature inside exactly right, all the food she wanted within reach. No trauma at all in being lifted off, as good as being lifted in Dr. Lavel's arms. Decide that weightlessness is more blessing than curse. Believe that those on Earth are thinking not so much of measurements and controls, but of her well-being as she rockets farther and farther away from them. She always liked night, anyway. Decide that there will be someone to meet her on the other side, someone as kind and patient as Dr. Lavel, and when she looks back at Earth, she won't think about any of the years on the street, or those first nights in the lab, but only about looking ahead. Seeing what's next.

2010 | What is it that makes us turn away from the grieving?

Language fails. No one wants to say the wrong thing. Grief is a monster. Grief laughs at language, lazy language, its tendency to tidy, order, sweeten, console. "It's all part of the deal." Or: "You'll meet again in another place." Bullshit. It's quite possible you could say such a thing and never mean to say it, never know where it was coming from.

Or is our aversion more animal than that? Is it a set about the eyes? The way they hold their mouths? Maybe it is a smell they give off, a sadness collecting in their hair. A smell of motor oil, basement, rotten leg of lamb, an oil burner gone wrong, and if we breathe it we won't ever get that smell out of our nostrils. We fear that if we're around them too much, some of their bad smell will put a spell on us, and we'll lose everything that's dear to us, too. We'll lose our friends and families; we'll lose our houses. And of course we'll do a much worse job of it. Oh, we'll be completely raw in our grief, crawling around on our hands and knees until our palms are worn. We won't be able to get up off the ground. And no one will call our phones or drop off baked goods because we were always too self-oriented to think about anyone else.

Maybe it isn't so sweeping. Maybe coming into contact with such immensity helps us to see that our lives are small, full of the dullest tasks made to distract us from the inevitable: we're all walking up the road to death. We can't hold on to that image without turning away from it. Virginia Woolf gets it right when she writes, "Bridges would cease to be built. Roads would peter off into grassy tracks . . ."

Today everyone—M, my good friends, everyone—is involved in their busy lives. I say that with as much neutrality as I can. I haven't made myself available to anyone exactly. I'm a visiting professor at a university, and I'm mentoring four graduate students from another university. If I had a grant or a fellowship, if I didn't have to go into work to lead my classes or meet my students, I'm sure I'd leave the house less and less, only forcing myself to the supermarket when the coffee situation required attention. I know I'm certainly guilty of staying away from others when they needed me most. Not deliberately, but it is so easy to put off that phone call to the next day.

We wait for the day when that friend has turned toward other things. No longer weighed down with the leaden coat of grief, and back to everyday anxieties: what to make for dinner, or what to do about jury duty.

I'm certainly not that person yet. After some good days, some good weeks really, I see a surprising feature on my skin as I step out of the shower. A constellation of pink and crimson welts. The band stretches from the middle of my chest, beneath the right nipple, around to the center of my backbone. It looks as if someone has taken a cigarette and burned me with it, strategically, to punish my nerve endings. The band is remarkably ugly, and I can't tell what's worse, the growing pain of the sores, or the way the sores make me feel about my body. There's been no warning for this, no headache or fever, no tingling or burning. It looks as if a war has played out on my skin. The inside of me rising against the outside. The sores weep. I thought I was doing so well, and now I see what I really am underneath it all: lost dog, wild and yowling, walking farther and farther into the woods.

"Look," I say to M an hour later. We're standing in the living room. At Roger and Jill's next door, someone is working a power saw. A mist of ripped wood is clouding the view beyond the fence. The sky looks like rain. I pull up my shirt to show him my torso.

"Ouch," he says, wincing. "Sweetheart. *Ouch*." He reaches out with his hand to touch—I know he wants to make it better—before he pulls back. "I'm sorry. What is it?"

"Shingles," I say.

"Shingles? What makes you say that?"

I walk over to the open laptop, where I show him the results of my research. The faces in the images look miserable; it's as if each of them has been exposed to a chemical blast. In one picture a man's forehead is scabbed from the middle of his cheek to his hairline. The swelling is so extreme that he can't open his left eye. We can't even look without screwing up our faces. I make a loud sound of disgust and close the laptop with a snap.

"You have to go to the doctor," M says. "I'm calling Dr. Steve."

I shake my head brusquely. I tell him there's no reason to go to Dr. Steve when I've already made an accurate diagnosis. I don't want to go to Dr. Steve. He is simply going to tell me to stay home and rest as there is no treatment for shingles, just some medication to prevent it from getting worse, and I'm clearly past the initial stage where it could still be of use.

"If you're sick," he says, minutes later, "I don't think I'm going to be strong enough to take care of you."

M's voice is quiet now, thick with suppressed tears in his throat. Then he starts to cry. By sick, he means HIV-sick. It hadn't even occurred to me that shingles could be a sign of HIV. In three months I'll find out from Dr. Steve that I've tested negative, but right now I want to say, you *could* take care of me, I promise. I wouldn't be that much work.

I just want to be held. That is the one and only thing I need right now. But I don't know how to ask for his arms around me, even though we've been together fifteen years. I might just be afraid that he'll hug me for two minutes out of obligation and get on with his day.

Later that afternoon, I turn on the Weather Channel to see Washington's Mount Rainier practically filling up the screen. Then another view of the mountain from the street of a featureless subdivision, another from the waters of Puget Sound, then one more from a tourist town with a coffee shop, a fruit stand, a gas pump, an organic food store. Boys skateboard through the haze of an unseasonably hot day. Haze against snow: it's all a little nauseating. The voice-over says, *Not* if *It Will Happen,* but *When.* Then footage of a young couple walking briskly to a hillside to avoid the onslaught. Then a chart graphing the buildup of roiling matter beneath the poised, boreal mountain.

I get a kick out of the visual dramatizations, which is probably the unspoken wish of the producers and directors: they don't really want to scare us. Pieces of rock belt the air, the atmosphere is impenetrable. But I'm especially mesmerized by the sluice of melted snow, lava swamping the streets to the eaves of the houses. You could say it's the color of chocolate milk or mocha, but it's not so appealing as that.

Bury it, I think. The whole fucking lot of it. Ugly houses and their vain yearnings.

I walk back to the bathroom, pull up my shirt, and study myself again. Shingles. What am I, old now? For the next month I'll check myself every few minutes just to make sure I'm not leaking lava.

Sometimes Relationships That Didn't Happen Are Worse Than the Ones That Did

1985 | It must be nearly eleven when Denise calls me one Tuesday night, in spring. "I'll take it in the den," I say to my father after he's already answered the phone. My father's voice always turns gruff once he figures out Denise is calling. The truth is she calls a lot, two times a day, sometimes for two or three hours at a time. Calls to our house are met with a busy signal, a harsh warning sound. Do I like being on the phone so much? The question doesn't occur to me. Denise is in my life, and this is part of the pact. And what must my father think when he walks into his den to see me lying on the bare floor, drawing air pictures with my finger? My face might seem to be a little blissed, as if Joni is singing her newest song only for me. I'm not speaking at all. There isn't space for me to speak, which must prompt my father to think: what could this divorced woman, this single mother, want with my son? He's seen her picture on the inner flap of her book. A glamour shot: half-parted mouth, a smart, but plainly sexual look in her eyes. She looks a little wounded, sexually wounded, actually, but there's hauteur there, too: she is not someone to be messed with. She's been places, if not literal places. She has the face of an actress, and perhaps that's why he steps right over me, without apology or acknowledgment, to retrieve some file about the proposed condo project he's been fighting across the lagoon from our summerhouse.

I'm not sure why I'm not fazed by his gruffness. Maybe it's simply because I like his den, the no-nonsense masculinity of it: the hard edges, the solid desk, the metal lamp with its dark bronze hood. No pictures on the walls but a serene-spooky Jesus, with a dog-like face, and a band of thorns twisting into a sore, liver-colored heart. I dreamed of this Jesus as a child. I was sitting before him, listening to his mellifluous voice, when a man sprang out of the crowd and shot him in that holy heart. I woke up panting with two hands covering my own heart, and minutes must have gone by before I was back to myself again.

Not long before she dies, Denise mentions that she was always afraid to stay on the line whenever my father picked up the phone. And she laughs when she tells me that. She was afraid he'd be harsh with her, interrogate her. The deadly seriousness of that voice. And I'm amazed to think she had the nerve to keep calling.

Tonight she's reading to me from the New Novel. She's been working on the New Novel since not long after the *Good Deeds* pub party. This book is a lot different from that book: longer, more elaborate sentences. The central character is a writer of children's books named Emily. Emily has a very young daughter named Lizzie. The husband, Peter, dies unexpectedly of a heart attack. And most important, there's a playwright. This playwright, Gene, rents the second floor of Emily's house, on a beach block in a beach town based on Ocean City, after coming upon an ad she'd put up in the supermarket. The playwright takes an interest in Emily's work. The playwright gets to know Emily; he takes an interest in Lizzie. You know where this leads.

The book pivots on one line: "sometimes relationships that didn't happen are worse than the ones that did."

I listen to a new page of the book every night. I try to get as many freshman comp papers graded as I can before Denise calls, but if I'm not done by the time she calls, I don't mind. So I'll wake up an hour earlier in the morning, so what? Listening to Denise is my real education. And besides, Denise is much more interesting than writing EXAMPLE? or CLARITY? in the margin of some comparison-contrast essay.

At first I am startled by what a terrible listener I am. It isn't like watching a movie. And it is certainly not like reading. When I read, I'm so prone to stopping midsentence; my attention pools in empty space, and the floaters in my eyes drift down the wall until the next sentence pulls me back in. Denise doesn't know it, but it can sometimes take me five minutes to get through a single page. Over the phone, her sentences speed past me like meteors, and I can feel Denise listening to me as I'm listening to her. By that I mean she is listening for laughs, pauses, silences after lines that are supposed to be jokes. She is listening for changes in my breathing. The enormity of this responsibility wipes me out sometimes. I stare fixedly at the paperweight on my father's desk so I won't get distracted, to anchor my attention.

The book starts, stalls, starts again, as all books do. Should it be in first person? Third? How many points of view? Denise seems determined to develop the language. She wants multifaceted sentences, rich with description and sound, that echo the books she loves: *Tender Is the Night, The Stranger, Madame Bovary, Ghost Dance.*

I see how a book becomes your house. But soon you are just a function of your house. The house tells you what you want, how you should live. At the same time, everything that comes into your life goes into the house. The house transforms the ordinary into the extraordinary, and without it, you'd never even know yourself, never even know that all those choices and consequences mattered. Your life has purpose inside that house, in its moldings and floorboards, in the way the light falls on the windowsill, and you pass on that house to others.

One day we take the hour drive to Ocean City, the Buick too wide for the lanes of the causeway. Austen, Denise's six-year-old daughter, sits up in the backseat, studying the whitecaps on the bay, the blue power plant at Beesley's Point. We're here to find Emily's house. For Denise, the task is not so much about finding the house that would be right for Emily as it is an act of attention, finding the house that's always existed. But before we find that house, we park.

We walk the boardwalk, scrubbed and bright on this cold spring day. Waves boom against the shoreline. They retreat and break once again, this time with the sound of a whip crack. We smell the ions in the air. There is a triumph about the three of us moving as one, the sights ahead of us—the Music Pier, Wonderland, Gillian's Fun Deck—calling up old stories. A woman walks by, mystified, alarmed by us. Ocean City is comfortable. Looking at it the way we're looking at it? Well, that would be like looking at your aunt Barbara as if she were the most wondrous creature on the planet, when in fact she's just Aunt Barbara, with her loose cardigans and her wide hips. But we're liked here, too. Others smile at us; they seem to want to be taken in by our laughter. They want to play along. I'm positive they're mistaking Denise and me for a happy couple with their daughter— the wonders that await the happy heterosexual couple with their daughter! Don't I feel it, a new stature accorded to me? I feel the swagger in my walk and talk. When we step inside Litterer's, for instance, we're directed to a table close to the boardwalk, as if we're some centerpiece of fertility.

We drive up and down the streets. One three-story is almost right for Emily but is immediately discarded for its vinyl siding. Another fails to make the grade because it is too close to busy West Avenue: bad for Lizzie, who likes to push her toys about the yard. We drive past the houses of the Gardens, with their suburban land-scaping and surgically edged driveways. We drive past the Port-O-Call, near where Grace Kelly and her family once summered, but that's not right either: Emily values trees, charm, wood shingles, and tradition—a smart, studied mess. Everything we've come across is blocky and practical. More than once we think Emily would never get any writing done in such a place, even though Nan and Gay Talese spend summers here. Maybe Emily would find Ocean Gate—the city based on Ocean City—deadening, stultifying. Maybe the Ocean City that Denise wants to exist doesn't exist. She wants a perfected ver-sion of the perfected imagination of her childhood, just as Emily is a perfected version of Denise, even if she doesn't think of Emily as having come from her. She doesn't claim ownership of Emily, Lizzy, or Gene; that would be wrong. It's as if they've already been fully formed, birth to death, outside of time. And that is as close to religion as Denise gets.

We're headed down Atlantic Avenue now, drifty, overheated, probably a little exhausted from having spent so much time with each other. We're already talking about coming back another day, when there's no school prep waiting for us, no front on the horizon—see the swollen blue clouds coming in from the bay side? We've left our heavy coats at home. We're probably wearing sneakers and our feet are numb. Then, when we're not trying, we see it. On the ocean side, at Fourth Street. An old lifesaving station? Yes, from the late nineteenth century, without a hint of Cape May twee. It's sided in a pale butter color, with barn-red trim. It suggests rigor, understatement; it can already foresee the Arts and Crafts movement. The house is beloved but not fussed with. There are bare patches on the lawn, bushes withered from the salt air. (Can't we also imagine Lizzie's toys strewn about the yard? Soggy bathing suits and towels hanging on the line?) It is the house of someone who has been places, who has lived in New York or San Francisco or London and come back home, not because it was Aunt Barbara, but because there was an extraordinary house here, a house that still pulses with the looking of everyone who's passed by it, who's dreamed through its red front door.

We park the car. We walk toward the ocean. We step across Corinthian Avenue, take in the view of the beach, Emily's beach, where Lizzie digs with her hands through clean gray sand. We turn back. We listen to what she'd hear from her front porch: a talk show on the TV, KYW Radio: All News All the Time. A high school kid tossing newspapers onto yards. We don't say very much. We look up at the house where Gene will betray Emily. We stand there long enough until a face appears at the second-floor window of the house next door. If we could translate that expression into a sentence, it would say, *who are these aliens and what do they want?* Then we get back in the car.

2010 | I sit closer to the stereo speakers, as if by leaning into them I'll hear better. I click past the first track to the second. It is a winter day. I wait for the lyrics as the song builds, grows into itself. The song is a tree now; it shakes when birds pass through it. The song gets a little calmer when the wind stops blowing its branches. The song is for Denise—or at least about Denise, according to DyAnne, Denise's other best friend. DyAnne has sent me the CD, and I stare at the guts of the padded envelope I've torn apart, hastily. Not so many years ago, the writer and singer of the song—DyAnne's fellow band member, and is it brother?—dated Denise. A rock musician dating Denise? Why didn't she ever tell me? Did she think I might not have been supportive of that, her taking up with a fellow artist? I had been privy to so much, to the details of sexual encounters and fallings out with close friends, and she's an enigma all over again. I never knew her. Do I feel just a flash of betrayal? Well, yes.

M walks into the living room carrying an armful of cut willows. "Listen," I say, gesturing at the stereo speaker. "Hear that?"

"What's that?" M says.

I tell him the band is Smash Palace. I tell him it's the song that was written for Denise, about Denise.

M stops his hunt for the suitable vase: pale green or gray? He's looking into the room, eyes fixed on nothing, as entranced as I am. He's taking the song in, or perhaps he's been thinking about that poem he's been meaning to write. He's been as drifty as I am lately, and I can't seem to pin him down.

"Sit," I say, patting the empty spot beside me on the sofa. "You have to hear it from the beginning, the whole song."

He puts the willow branches down, sits. He stretches out his long legs on the coffee table. "How are the shingles?" he says, pulling up my T-shirt.

"They say hello," I say. "Thank you for thinking of us." And I pull my shirt back down.

We listen. We press our knees into each other's knees. I feel the warmth of his skin coming into my skin. The tree of the song is shaking again. We both look at each other, brows tightening, mouths loose. "He loved her," we both say in the same voice.

1985 | B, the English professor, asks Denise out on a date. B takes her out on another. He takes her to nice restaurants, he buys her beautiful things. He talks of taking her to Paris, which he's sure she'll fall in love with. Now that she's no longer his student, he can tell her everything, what it's like to see that face, that shining face, not only beaming out toward the others in the seminar room, but toward him, whenever he tried to challenge her in class. She wouldn't back down, unlike the others, who were too afraid or polite, and that was beautiful to him. The ferocity of intelligence that deepened the brown in her eyes! Not to mention the sweet and sexy husk in her voice.

But his face turned toward her? She's not quite having it, not quite. The lavishness of attention is all a little much. She thinks it wants her essence, even though he tells her he wants nothing but to be with her, to talk about books with her. She'd prefer some mystery, some elusiveness, and—does she admit it to herself?—some hardness and indifference. A prize she has to win. She is not anyone's prize, no gilded starling high on a shelf. Over and over she tells me, he's not the one, he's not the one. She is waving her hands around; we are walking down Walnut Street, heading toward Rittenhouse Square. I'm trying to nod, I'm trying to listen, to be of support to my friend. Maybe if I point out that baby in her father's arms, she'll be shaken out of herself and her blood pressure will go back down again. But on and on she goes, as if by resistance she becomes stronger, larger. Resistance straightens her back; resistance lifts up her chin, brings a smolder to her mouth and chin and eyes.

Months later, on a peaceful Wednesday night in spring, Denise tells me she is marrying B.

She tells it to me again, as if by doing so, she'll vaporize the hundreds of hours I've spent listening to her saying no, no, no.

My face might color. Certainly the space just above my nose is so hot that it must be the color of raw meat. How could she not have betrayed a hint of their relationship during all those three-hour phone calls? I'd understand it better if she'd wandered away from me. The secrecy of it feels a little like lying. And this has been going on for, what—six months? I thought she wanted to be single.

She structures her explanation with the logic of a trial lawyer, but she's not working too hard. She doesn't expect me to be a hostile judge. After all, I haven't yet lost my temper or grimaced or frowned. Would I ever lose my temper with her? Probably not, and maybe this frustrates her. This is what she wants of me, though she can't quite say it. How would she tell a friend to get mad at her? I know she's not getting married simply to raise my hackles, that would be flat-out absurd, but maybe my calm, accepting face is not the face she wants right now. If a friend is simply someone who says yes, everything you do is all right, well, maybe that's not really a friend.

But maybe I'm being too hard on myself. I could also say that a real friend loves his friend enough to let her wander. He lets her drive off the road, down into the muck, if she has to. He does not push or possess. He is not bossy or parental. He waits for that friend to come back to herself, to him. He's standing at the top of the stairs for her, with a neutral, expectant face. He takes her hand when she extends it up to him.

Denise: a woman whose heroines are Emma and Cathy. She invited me to build a fortress with her. Here I was, hefting stone columns on my back, and now she's telling me there's never been a house to build?

Maybe it is a relief that the dream of Famous Writer is over. Goddamn Famous Writer and everything he represented: East

Hampton, literary ambition, dinners with the rich, always running around, always giving readings, sleeping with acolytes and admirers. She must have come to some revelation in Vermont. She must have seen it in his hectic face: he wasn't a happy man. If anything, his work was a bear that was hunting him down. It lurked behind trees, it lurked outside barns in the form of a woman. It made him dial a number in the middle of the night, and hang up the phone before that same woman on the other end answered, just so he'd feel stirred up enough to write another page, the page of the book that doesn't yet exist, even though he's been paid hundreds of thousands of dollars for it. I cannot blame Denise for wanting to replace him with a healthier ideal. At least with B, she'll have a life of steadiness, calm, domestic routine. She'll be able to write. Teach, but she won't have to teach too much. Spend relaxed time with Austen, who deserves health care, a good room, good clothes, the best education.

Or maybe we just need to knock down those old ideals before they knock us down first.

2010 | I'm lying on the living room sofa, watching a video of Atlantic City's Sands Hotel on YouTube. The view is from the boardwalk. It's going to be blown up in minutes. The demolition firm has made a party of it, with fireworks, a crowd of thousands, and the soundtrack of Frank Sinatra crooning "Bye, Bye Baby." Some clever PR person was smart to pick Sinatra, given the fact that he was regular here. Word had it that management actually knocked through the walls of several side-by-side rooms to save him the trouble of walking down the hall. The twenty-year-old hotel hosted his final concerts, in which he reportedly wasn't in top form. Still, he sang with enough conviction to make up for the exhaustion in his voice, those occasional moments when his pitch faltered or he mumbled through a phrase.

My rash hasn't gone away after a week. In fact, it's gotten worse. There's a hot-pins-and-needles feeling around my ribs and a general malaise that's preventing me from doing anything of meaning or purpose. I know my body might be telling me that it's had enough of death, of trying to float on its chilly surface, and maybe there's a relief in saying, *no, I'm not going to resist you any longer. I'm giving in to you, Force that wants to take down my body.* Maybe there's a lesson to be learned from obedience, submission. All the stamina I'd poured into meeting my classes, meeting my appointments, meeting my deadlines—who did I think I was? Did I think I was better at holding back sorrow than anyone else who had lost anybody? Mourning as some kind of graduate school assignment where some got better grades than others? Have I been thinking of myself as Superman, walking into the world with my cape, without even knowing I was wearing a cape? If I were looking at myself, wouldn't I find that person a little pitiable, ridiculous?

Still, it is hard to give in, to *relax,* as they say, when your tolerance for boredom is low. Wet snow clumps on the lilac outside the window. I don't have to be anywhere for days, having already canceled my classes for the next week and five college readings in Florida—what a time to be sick. I let my mind drift in the heat put out by the furnace, the crackling wood stove, the hazy malaise of shingles. How am I going to get anything done when I'm frittering away the hours, speeding from one YouTube video to the next?

The crowd presses toward the boardwalk railing. They watch the emptied tower shoot plumes from the roof, before the whole structure shimmers in a bilious green light. It's the definition of spectacle: the crowd hoots and hollers; adults and children hold cell phones and cameras up to the rockets. Maybe they know the building better than I do. Maybe at least some of them have wandered its hallways and found it wanting. Truth be told it was the hardest casino to like. Always a little doomed, dark, never flashy or distinctive enough. The building could have been anywhere: Cincinnati, Bakersfield, Tampa, Anaheim, Phoenix. It would be foolish to think it was anything to mourn. I remind myself of that when someone in the crowd cries, with a lusty growl, "Take it down, baby. Take the whole ugly thing down."

But the light changes after the fourth minute of the video. Its brilliance only ends up illuminating the space where the windows once were, and the rocketing fireworks feel desperate—ecstasy can only be sustained for so long. And can I be the only one who is thinking of war now? We are watching the ongoing, meaningless war (Iraq, Afghanistan) that the culture turns into entertainment.

Then everything stops, stills. A puff of smoke shoots up from the roof. The crowd is hungry. Three hundred fifty pounds of dynamite—what else should we expect of ourselves?

And just like that it's gone. But the way it comes down? It comes down as a person would, balancing there for a minute, stricken. It takes a twist to the left, as if a leg had given way, and falls on its back. I take it personally.

Famous Writers

1986 | The phone rings in my parents' kitchen on a Thursday morning, sometime in the middle of March. My hello might not be in my actual voice, the voice I use to talk to my parents, but a little deeper, more serious. I don't know why I talk to Denise in that huskier register, and I don't spend any time questioning it. Denise will be done teaching for the week after one o'clock, and maybe we will take a drive to Avalon and Cape May.

It isn't Denise on the phone, but the administrator of the writers conference. The administrator is calling to tell me I'm being offered a working scholarship, which means I'll be waiting tables at the conference, in exchange for room and board and tuition.

By waiting tables we mean waiting on Famous Writers.

"Do you think you'd like to do that?" says the administrator.

Is my name Paul Lisicky? Is—"I think I'm going to cry," I say dizzily, after a dense, awkward patch.

"Please don't do that," she says, with a frown inside her voice.

"Okay, then I'll just run around the house twenty times and wag my tail."

That makes her laugh, which makes me laugh. She gives me the details of what will be expected of me—ten days, three meals a day. But I'm not taking very much of it in. It doesn't so much matter to me that waiting tables and attending classes and craft talks and readings isn't exactly a vacation; all I know is that the working scholars have the best time. They're in the spotlight; they give their own group reading. They're taken in by everyone, because some of the best-known writers were once waiters. And besides, doesn't everyone love someone who's straining at the gate, waiting to rush forward?

I call Denise instantly. I want to tell her first, even before I tell my parents.

She picks up. I tell her that she isn't going to believe what she's about to hear.

She must squeal, she must scream—I know she must. But two seconds beyond that, I can't remember a thing about our conversation. I can't remember whether she's telling me who to say hello to. I can't remember whether she's telling me who to stay away from. Surely she must be giving me tips about the weather, the mix of hot and cold—one minute it's eighty-seven, the next a cloud comes over the mountain and you're shivering in your barn coat, hands shoved in your pockets.

My mind is drifting toward my image of that mountain, which looks lethal in its power, like my idea of Mont Blanc, which I discuss in a thirty-page bullshitty paper I've just written on Shelley's spirituality. Up to this point my work has only been seen by Denise, by my teacher Lisa Zeidner, and the students in Lisa's workshops. What will it mean to have my work seen by people who don't know me, people to whom I haven't already said supportive things?

If I hear any envy in Denise's voice, I respond by pretending it's not there. If she doesn't hear any confusion or guilt in me, then she'll know there's no reason for her to feel left out. Competition will not be real if I decide we're to be above all that.

Is that what I'll do for the next twenty-some years of our friendship?

And maybe that's why she says, with a hardness I've never heard before, "I'm not going back until I'm faculty. Full faculty."

2010 | Why is my memory so patchy? Why can't I remember better from those times? It infuriates me. All I have are fragments, bursts of sound and taste and color.

If you asked me what I did in 2001, I'd say M and I lived for a semester on the thirteenth floor of a high-rise in the heart of Greenwich

Village. I'd say our golden retriever, Beau, died after a two-year-long bout with kidney disease. Say we drove his blanket-wrapped body up to the Provincetown house, where we buried him in the front yard, as Arden, his older brother, watched solemnly, paws crossed out in front of him, by the edge of the pit M dug. Say we bought a one-bedroom apartment on West Sixteenth Street. Say we moved into that apartment exactly a week before the towers fell, before we had a TV or any furniture except for a bed. Say that I was afraid to breathe too deeply lest the dust (bones? ground-up plastic?) get trapped in my lungs. Say restaurants were still serving people on sidewalk tables in December: the warm weather wouldn't let go in spite of the trauma in the atmosphere.

But if you asked me about what I was doing in the middle of the eighties? The middle of the eighties is a frozen hole, volcano deep. I had a pretty good record of leaving crappy jobs behind. I was afraid of becoming that kind of feckless young person who took a job then quit it instantly. But the bigger story was that I'd managed to finish my graduate degree in English. I'd brought a project to completion, but I was scared shitless about what was to come next. I wanted to become myself, but there wasn't even a self to work with. I went to the Cherry Hill Library to research editorial assistant jobs at the *Village Voice.* I dreamt about the men I never touched. I was in suspension mode, moving through my own life as a burglar might move through an empty house, with gloves on, careful not to leave any fingerprints behind.

And maybe that's why I don't remember a thing about Denise's wedding—the time of day or year. I think I might have played the guitar. Joey might have played the trumpet, but that might have been another wedding. I don't remember her dress, whether it was long or above the knee, white or not. Was there lace? Don't remember a thing about her vows. Or the reception afterward, talking to her parents, her sister, her brother, Austen—or even Lisa, who must have been there, too. Don't remember who sat at my table, whether it was an important table, or whether I was off in some corner, with the single, unattached people: the punishment table. Don't remember thinking that the days of long phone calls might be over, not to mention the nights of talking and making jokes till four in the morning.

2010 | Off the north coast of Haiti, the sea floor buckles. The coral reef rises through the surface; vast tracts of once-productive farms plunge. This has happened in all of a month, since the Port-au-Prince earthquake. The video I'm watching is shot from a small plane. The coral reef looks like a moldy green cauliflower head, a single oak grows a mile from the revised shoreline. It's already drowned, already salt-burned. The thinking goes that the Port-au-Prince fault, dormant for a hundred years when it flattened Kingston, will need to release pressure soon. It is not so far-fetched to think that the next quake will trigger a tsunami the size and scope of the Sri Lanka tsunami. The announcer relays this information in a voice both portentous and stagey, though he sounds as if he's trying to keep the staginess in check. It would take fifteen minutes to reach Jamaica, a half hour to reach Cuba, one hour to reach the coast of South Florida. As to whether a warning system is in place for such an event: Humans are pretty good at not learning from the mistakes that have already befallen us. We wouldn't be able to bear it if we'd braced ourselves for every possible disaster. We certainly know of people who live that way, staying away from skyscrapers when it's windy, walking across the street when they see a ladder, avoiding bridges at all costs lest the center lane collapse. Too much of that, though, and we wouldn't even leave the house in the morning. Maybe this is how people think who never leave their houses.

There's my eighty-six-year-old father on the sixth floor of his Fort Lauderdale condo, working for the third week in a row on his income tax. Would he listen to me if I called to tell him about the oncoming wave? Of course not. He'd remind me that he was high up from the sea, in a sturdy building that withstood Hurricane Rita.

(Or maybe it was Wilma. Rita or Wilma, he held the living room hurricane shutter closed with all his might as hundred-mile-per-hour winds sirened on the balcony.) Of course it would bother him that the minivan was down in the parking lot. Should he drive it across the bridge to the grocery store parking ramp? But, really, he saw no unusual activity out on Riverside Drive. It is August, and all the snowbirds and tourists are home in Montreal or Buffalo Grove or West Hartford. I'd try to think of other ways to convince him, but he'd finally tell me that he'd be all right, that there was no reason to worry about him.

1986 | It isn't like Denise to withhold a hello when she picks up the phone. Didn't I have a dark dream about her last night? Maybe I did: I'm in a balloon going up, the hot air heating the top of my scalp, singeing it. I almost can't stand it, the feeling is intimate. Cattle flee on the pasture beneath us. She's not making sense. The sound of her voice is the sound of a mouth that's been punched. Or, as if someone close to her, someone beloved to her—her mother, her father— has been pushed down a full flight of stairs, and she's been forced to watch.

She tells me that her editor's letter came in but five minutes ago. Her response to the new book, or at least the first draft.

"And?" I feel a tightness in my chest, but elation, too, inexplicably.

"She hates the novel."

"Denise."

"I'm serious, honey. I'm still trying to take this in. I think I'm still in a bit of shock. It's going to take me a little while to be myself again."

I ask her what Iris has said.

The letter is certainly not what any writer would want to hear. Iris is careful to start with the good things; she wants to assure Denise that she's responding to the novel in a careful, detached manner. But we can already hear the dutiful quality of the prose. It has no swing: this wasn't the letter she'd been wanting to write. In that way, the letter is hard to listen to; I can only take in so much of it. Especially when it gets parental. *You are not the child I'd been expecting you to be,* her words seem to say. And this from an editor who's been so fully on Denise's side? How could she love one child so, and treat the other as if its ears are ugly, its voice grating? Given how much I've listened to the book, I feel as if my advice is also under attack here, for Denise wanted to impress me in the writing of it. I so much want to say Iris doesn't know what the fuck she's talking about, but I know it would be wrong to explode like that. This is serious, scarier than it seems. Denise has already gotten an advance on the book, so she has to do what the mother of the book wants—no getting around that.

Luckily she isn't so devastated that she can't disagree with some of what Iris says. We go over and over what she takes issue with. We try to be grown up: too much is at stake here. We plan possible strategies that might placate Iris, without actually giving in. Maybe the book *is* Emily's book, maybe it should be in a closer third person. Maybe it moves through too many points of view, too many registers of voice to be comprehensible. Maybe Emily shouldn't die at the end of the book. Maybe it's too much a reach to suggest that Emily dies from heartbreak. "You are not that kind of writer," Iris writes. Is she implying that Denise's talents don't match her vision? No real writer feels like her talents match her vision, but Iris doesn't seem to want Denise to have grand ambitions. She seems to want Denise to write an accessible and pleasant book, maybe just a little off-kilter, a book the publicists can compare to Anne Tyler or Alice Hoffman. It will sell a reasonable number of copies, enough to make the bosses happy, so she can keep publishing books.

A woman's book.

In other words, do not think you are Monsieur Proust.

At some point Denise starts crying softly, very softly. It is barely audible. I imagine her holding the phone away from her face for a minute while I go on talking, doing my stupid best to say the right thing. And then she takes her hand off the mouthpiece.

The sentence Denise keeps coming back to concerns the novel's opening. Iris writes, "You have to earn an opening like that." Denise says it again, and after two minutes, she repeats it, this time with more molten rage.

From here, I can see that Iris might be talking about cause and effect, consequence. Iris might in fact be saying that the opening is too intense, too elaborate, with too many embedded clauses in the sentences, to be friendly to the reader.

The fact is this: Iris wants another *Good Deeds,* but a *Good Deeds* that sells more, gets more reviews, gets more attention for the other books on the list. She wants the writer and the book she fell in love with five years back, but one with all the nouns changed.

Denise, however, hears Iris's words differently, and maybe Denise knows what she's talking about. Denise believes Iris is telling her that she doesn't have the sophistication or education to write a sentence like that. Iris has an MFA from Iowa, just as Famous Writer, Flannery O'Connor, and Jayne Anne Phillips have MFAs from Iowa. Denise herself had wanted to go to Iowa, but stopped herself from putting the application in the mail even after she'd filled out the forms, filled out the check, sealed the envelope. I don't understand how you could want something so much that you'd make sure it wouldn't work out, but maybe I deal with that complexity by convincing myself the opportunity wasn't so great to begin with.

Denise, though, will never let go of her feeling and fury. Iris doesn't know she is dealing with a thunderstorm. Denise knows exactly what it is to please. And she will please Iris as if pleasing is a kind of murder.

With that in mind, Denise looks at the pages. She moves chapters around, pares back sentences to their essence. She makes Emily someone the reader can "identify with," as they say. She makes her "sympathetic." She makes the book linear. She stays up night after night, coffee on constant brew. Over the next few months she writes a simpler, more streamlined version of the book she'd wanted to write, a book she probably loves a little less, though she doesn't have it in her to say it to herself like that. But maybe that's a better place to write from: loving a little less. The new book is a replacement for the dream book. Others will never see the dream book, but she'll always have it in her head. It will pulse like a jellyfish, dangerous, blue, just out of reach, up in the sky rather than down, underwater. "If only—" she'll say years later, punishing herself for walking away from it.

Monster

1888 | Vincent loves Arles: the filth of it, the light, the brothels, even the people, who strike him as creatures from another world. The town is a bit of a backwater: a plus to him. Though he's been sick—smoker's cough and too much absinthe—he's been working well, paintings of yellow, ultramarine, and mauve, curled and slapped onto the canvas with a knife. He loves his Yellow House, where he's lived since leaving the Hotel-Restaurant Carrel, but happiness is missing. A friend is missing, other artists are missing. He has thoughts of founding a collective of artists, and when Gauguin promises to meet him in Arles, he buys two beds for the house and gets to work on his most ambitious paintings yet. He can't stop work, and he can't stop thinking of Gauguin, whose presence will change his life, change painting, as we know it. His friend's presence will challenge him; they'll argue fiercely about the things they care about. They'll draw closer to each other, and there won't ever be a reason to think they'll ever need to leave home.

But Gauguin has a different idea. He finally comes to Arles after repeated requests. Is he coming because he really wants to live and paint with Vincent, or is it because he feels hounded and it's just too hard to say no? He doesn't know, but he gives in one day. He arrives, sets up his easel, and within a matter of days, he's painting Vincent's portrait, *The Painter of Sunflowers.* He persuades Vincent to paint from memory, as he does, and in a matter of days they even embark on a collaborative work, an outdoor project at the Alyscamps.

But the closeness to Vincent is killing him. He can't stop himself from arguing with him; he's not even sure he believes in the points he's arguing for, but Vincent brings it out in him. Vincent is turning him into someone he isn't. Vincent is turning him into a monster, someone who wants to hurt Vincent, for Vincent is just waiting for Gauguin to desert him at any minute. How could Gauguin not be exhausted from it, those eyes always turned to him, those ears just waiting for that strain of formal speech, which Vincent will translate to: *I don't love you anymore.*

And even while these things are happening, they'll get the sense that the falling out isn't exactly of them, or inside them; it's out of their control. They've gotten hold of the notion that one person's success means the other's failure. For Gauguin, however, it's even more complicated than that—it is part of a deep internal knowing that he's not afraid to admit to. As much as he'd like to be brothers with Vincent, equally recognized by some hard but loving mother, that mother will always love one better. Currying the favor of the invisible mother: isn't that the essence of competition? And so Gauguin pulls away, which is why Vincent cuts his own earlobe. Or does Gauguin cut it, in a sword attack, in anger or self-defense, as some historians claim? Rather than turn his friend in, Vincent takes the ear to a prostitute and staggers home. His last written words to his estranged friend: "You are quiet, I will be, too."

1986 | I wait tables breakfast, noon, and dinner. I wait tables as if I've balanced trays and taken requests with a benevolent smile my whole life. I have a conversation with Francine Prose, who's not yet Francine Prose, about the work of Jane Bowles. I listen to Nancy Willard on the porch of the main house, trying not to rock my rocking chair too hard, trying to look in her face as if to reassure her that everything she says is helpful to me. She quotes John Gardner: "A decision to make a character a victim is disastrous." I try to store up everything she says while mosquitoes raise welts on my inner arm. I put so much effort into impersonating the look of the successful young writer of the day—J. Press shirts, Brooks Brothers grosgrain watchband, and Birdwell Beach Britches for swimming—that I can't even tell how much it's wearing me down. Perhaps germs are already brewing in me, like the coffee molecules brewing inside the urns in the dining hall. I'm not exactly shocked when I come down with strep throat a week after my departure, as if my body would need to rebel, to lie on its back for two weeks.

But at every turn I'm thinking about Denise. Not just what I'll report back to her, but what I'll withhold from her: I don't want her to think I'm having too good a time. I look at the pond, and I remember a story she once told me about Mark Strand's dismissal of one student's work: "If I'd written a poem like this, I'd jump in the pond." I look up at the podium in the theater and wish she were here to listen to Tim O'Brien, whom she always refers to as Tim, though I don't think she's ever met him. It occurs to me that I'm looking and listening for two people. My appreciation for the cloud passing over the mountain is her appreciation as well, but it's hard to split oneself in half like that. Is she wondering about me back where she is in South Jersey, where it must be humid today, where there must already be a kind of melancholy on the air? Summer is almost over, sweaters are on the shelves, and you couldn't find a folding beach chair in the hardware store, even if you bribed the clerk to go looking for one in the stock room.

I am afraid of saying the wrong thing. But I can also sense that it will be hard to keep the wrong thing trapped.

I think of Famous Writer. That space in front of the Barn is always the space of Famous Writer, even though he hasn't been back in years, and I walk past that zone warily as if he might leap out from behind the bushes.

I make friends. That's not so hard to do. There is a woman named Julie, who recently graduated from Cornell. She is tiny and sarcastic, with a clipped cranberry-colored Manic Panic bob. She looks like Edith Piaf might have looked if she were young now and listened only to the Smiths, New Order, Style Council, and the Cure. Like me, she likes to laugh, but she always has a sad look in her eye, as if she already knows too well that her life will not work out like others might want it to. I like her writing, especially the descriptions in her writing, which have a liveliness and snap to them. It seems to me that everything should be lined up for her. She could be a star. She seems to know that too well about herself, which might be why she's wary of all that. When it's time for the waiters to play volleyball, a requirement of sorts, we slink off from the others, sit beneath a pine, and talk about Susan Minot's *Monkeys*, the collection of the moment, not sure whether we approve of it or not. We also wonder who might and might not be gay, though I know very well to keep my mouth shut about myself.

I'm in my room one night. Everyone around me seems to be having sex. People tiptoe down fire escapes onto the lawn long after midnight, people have sex in the woods, in their coats, lying in cold, wet leaves. Even a fellow waiter who was just married two weeks before is leaning into the shoulder of another Famous Writer in the Barn, as if they've already gone to bed, or are planning to fuck any minute. Sex is expected of us, sex is charging up the air, but what would my roommate, admittedly a very nice guy, a runner and a wonderful writer, think if he knew I thought about dick a hell of a lot more than he did? Maybe he already knows that I think a lot about dick, which is why another waiter walks in one night, pounds on my stomach while I'm lying on the bed and cries, who are you going to fuck tonight? I laugh uproariously, as if by doing so I'm taking away the sting of the accusation, or the demand inside it. I know he is certainly not talking about fucking anything with a dick, for the message is clear: to be part of the group you must like chicks.

One day I see Michael Cunningham, who isn't yet Michael Cunningham of *The Hours*. He is standing along the windows, in the aisle of the theater. His arms are crossed over his chest; his face is glowing, tanned, sympathetic, wry, alert. He is pretending he is not being watched by everyone in the room when in fact he knows he is. At that moment he is the handsomest man I've ever seen. He looks like someone who knows his reaction is important; he knows we're more likely to steal looks at him instead of the polite reader of the polite work who's standing behind the podium. Later I tell him that I'm a fan of his first novel. I tell him that I know Denise, as he and Denise have the same editor. But do I let on that I'm attracted to men? Of course not. And he doesn't let on anything about himself either. That is the contract of the day, and we agree to it without realizing what we're giving up, simply because we, too, want to be standing behind that podium up front. And not only that, we want a place at the table, the head table, but we can't yet conceive of doing that if we let on that there are concurrent lives going on in our heads.

On the day of our departure, Julie and I fall into each other's arms and weep. We weep and weep, though our weeping is soundless. We don't shake. Hot tears soak into the shoulders of our T-shirts. Everyone around is loading up their cars, standing outside them with folded arms: all these people we'll never see again. We begin to laugh at ourselves, but we don't look each other in the face lest we start crying all over. I think we know that our friendship is only bound to this moment, that it would be impossible to sustain it with such intensity, with me in New Jersey and her in Baltimore.

Besides, I am already tied to someone.

Furious

In the mid-1980s Joni Mitchell wants us to know that her search for love is over. After years of relationships coming together and falling apart, she wants to let us know, through her music at least, that she's married and met her match. In theory this is a good thing. If only those happy songs—"We got this solid love"—could stand up next to the more complicated songs. Denise and I probably want to like these songs more than we do. It's not that we want Joni to be miserable. It's just that the positive feeling behind those happy songs is so absolute. Where are the oppositions, the nuance, the ambivalence, "the hope and hopelessness of thirty years"? The new songs almost spit cheerfully in the faces of the troubled songs that have preceded them, the troubled songs we've been identifying with. They say, that Joni? Well, that Joni was screwed up, selfish; she just wanted too much. She was unlucky in love. She made bad choices, she gave herself away to childish, narcissistic men. Denise and I are willing to entertain that. But it's confusing to have identified love with trouble for so long, and now we're supposed to think of love as pure.

Then another album comes out. The album opens with one of our favorites, "Good Friends," a love song that doesn't appear to be troubled by sexual tension. Sure, the two friends have their disagreements, but their love takes care of them in the end. But the other songs on the album make me nervous. They're hard songs, angry songs, songs about the environment, songs against war and capitalism and advertising—all the right causes—but they're as subtle as billboards, with none of the singular chord progressions and harmonic leaps that make Joni's songs what they are. They're external songs; they don't enact inquiry, a mind at work; they already know what they think before they start, before she even writes them. In that way they sound like the songs of someone who's trying to write a Joni song.

The question keeps ticking after so many years: if she is so happy, then why are these songs so pissed off?

Or maybe that isn't fair. On one level she doesn't want to repeat what she's done again and again. In that way, she's a model for any artist who reinvents herself over time. But it's impossible not to hear these songs without hearing her husband's influence, the straight-forward harmonic progressions, the blocky synthesizer chords, the overbright sound of the day. He's all over the album, from his face on the cover, to his name as songwriter, even though Thomas Dolby has been credited as producer. I don't doubt that he's a nice guy, you can see it in his face. To be honest, he reminds me a little bit of myself, with his long lashes, his big nose, the short space between that nose and his upper lip. His tendency to smile and please—it's all there. It's good that Joni has somebody to care for her, but it's unnerving to see her give up so much of herself when she shares the stage with her husband. How willingly she lets go of her boundaries, allowing herself to be subsumed, even when that husband probably doesn't want to subsume her. Yes, she is mad about the rain forest and mad about televangelists and the possibility of nuclear annihilation—no one in his or her right mind isn't—but there have to be other reasons why the songs are so goddamn furious.

1987 | In theory, Denise now has the relationship that should enable her to concentrate on her writing. A husband who gives her time to herself, a husband who believes in the project of her writing and wants it to be seen and taken in by serious readers. A writer him-self, he is getting attention for his nonfiction. Competition couldn't be further from his mind. He travels at every opportunity; he gives talks at colleges, gives interviews on radio and television, works as a language consultant to corporations. He's making money, doing what he can to give the three of them a good life. Denise could be writing. Denise *should* be writing. Instead, she spends much of her time thinking about a table.

If only she had the right writing table, Denise thinks, she'd be able to sit still for more than minutes at a time; she'd be able to work with fervor and fury on the novels, stories, and essays waiting to be written. The table cannot be a new table. The table must possess the aura of generations coming to life around it. She knows, in part, that her reasoning is absurd. She already has a study that most other writers would kill for, in a quiet room upstairs, far from the noise of the road. But the search for a table consumes weeks, months.

One day, my mother and I stand outside the family summer-house to greet Denise and Austen. They are coming to visit for the day. Our Boston terrier tears three times around the back lawn before Austen leans over to pick her up. Pebbles's eyes are startlingly wide; she's panting and frantic, but it's a happy frantic. In truth it must be a relief for my mother and Denise to lay eyes on each other, to spend time together, to find out that they like each other. We ask my mother if she'd like to join us at the boardwalk, but she says no. She says she has to go out to the store to buy food for dinner. *You don't have to make dinner, Anne,* Denise says. My mother says, *Oh, I want to make dinner.* Denise says, *Do you want me to help? Do you want us to bring some fish back?* My mother is stirred up with the prospect of this joint project.

She is quick to make jokes that aren't afraid of a little irreverence, as if she wants to let Denise know that she isn't dead to the fun parts of herself. It is the quality that always drew my friends to my mother. It is the quality that said, don't think of me as a mother, anything but that. I am your friend, your equal. And maybe on a certain level her offer to cook is a way to apologize to the woman she'd spent a considerable number of hours mistrusting, embroiled in some kind of imagined rivalry.

I don't remember if we stop by Emily's house before we walk the boardwalk. Certainly we must, even though Austen, who's in the backseat, must be eager to ride the rides, and eat every nasty thing one could possibly eat on a boardwalk: cotton candy, Copper Kettle Fudge, Mack and Manco pizza. I imagine the three of us getting out of the car; maybe I'm even holding Austen's hand, which might be warm and pleasantly sticky. We circle the yellow house three times, as if the three of us can imagine sharing it, hanging our laundry on the back line to dry, heating up water in a teakettle inside. And in doing that, we almost forget that it's not Emily's house, but our own.

Then we are up on the boardwalk. I'm eager to try out the roller coaster, which has always been my favorite ride, even though I haven't been on one in years. Austen, however, has a different idea. She wants to go on the Tilt-A-Whirl. We buy the tickets, and Austen pulls me up the ramp. In all my years of going on rides I have never been on a Tilt-A-Whirl. The operator lowers the bar across our waists. We hold on to the bar, to each other. It's been so long since I've been on rides that I've forgotten I don't do well with spinning around, and the Tilt-A-Whirl not only spins around but whips and lurches, jerking us from side to side. The two of us are laughing, squeezing our eyes shut, bare knees banging into each other. But this feeling in my head and stomach—isn't this experience supposed to be gentle? I'm not talking salt and pepper shakers, rides that throw you down only to whip you back up again. My stomach is increasingly displeased. There's nothing remotely fun about this. As for the sublimity of the scarier rides? We're not meeting our deaths, oh no. No imaginary confrontation with the angel or the monster. I'm just reminded that I have a body that's capable of being shaken while Austen laughs and laughs into my shoulder.

Denise waves at us the second the ride stops. Perhaps she's been waving at us the whole time, her smile bigger than I've ever seen it. Somehow I make it down the ramp without throwing up or falling down. I stand still for a second, but that is not the best cure. Better to simply walk down the boardwalk, pretend that I'm feeling reasonably all right without bumping into rails, people. The sun is boring into the tops of our heads, the bridges of our noses. We're in that pleasant, woozy state of mind when we don't feel any pressure to fill up the silence. And later, back at the house as the sun goes down, we'll eat our spaghetti out on the deck, looking out at the lagoon, while the usually rattled Boston terrier falls asleep, snoring, on Austen's left foot.

2010 | By 8 a.m., I've tweeted about loggerhead sea turtles in Cape Hatteras, bears sunning themselves in suburban Los Angeles, happy potbellied pigs in Brooklyn, and plundered sea cucumbers in Mexico. I am perfectly content to find stories of animals. It is my morning project, the first thing I do after a first sip of coffee. I'll find a few more links before I go to bed tonight. I scan dozens of news sites until my eyes are tired, until I can't put off school prep any longer. I don't believe there's a one-to-one relationship between my animal project and Denise, though I wouldn't be telling the full truth if I didn't say my project took off around the time of her death. I love animals, but I have no grand purpose in mind. If my tweet about a rabbit makes you look more closely at a rabbit in a field: great. If it makes you look past a rabbit dish on a restaurant menu: even better. If not? I am not the rabbit police. It is the ritual of the search that's important to me, the steady absorbing quality of the sorting, posting, passing on. I disappear into my project, dream into the forms of the animals I think about. For a little bit, I'm a turtle then a bear then a pig towing a drowning man across a lake to safety. The baggage of my human skin is a little lighter on my bones. We hear enough about humans, don't we?

If I were twenty-three in 2010 and Denise were thirty, and we were both teaching assistants at Rutgers, I wonder if we would have become friends today. Probably. But would we have been on the phone three hours every night? I don't think so. I imagine us sitting side by side in a darkish coffee shop, our faces purpled in laptop light. I'm tweeting, Denise is scrolling through Facebook. We're in tattered armchairs, plum and gold, with holes in the upholstery.

The room smells of dust, burned coffee, baked goods, candle wax, and old wood. A handsome bearded skateboarder walks in, sets off the bells on the door. We check out his skinny green pants, his thick brown beard; our eyes flit down again. Denise writes to five Facebook friends she doesn't actually know: it's mindless, oddly appealing work. Her tapping fills this corner of the room. There is so much less wanting on her face. The need can be spread out among many people, whom she writes to once a month. If Caitlin isn't available, Denise can write to Johannes. I wouldn't have to count so much for her, and she wouldn't have to count so much for me. We feel the lightness of our arrangement, the freedom of movement.

From one friend we get immediacy, spontaneity, the exasperated voice, the shaken head, the occasional embrace. But the brain wants many friends, acquaintances. So much less to miss and mourn if there's always someone else to replace the one you lost. One kind word means exactly the same as another kind word. The sweet relief of it. And maybe the brain has always known what's best for us.

1987 | Who follows me out of the single gay bar outside Hyannis? He walks across the dark parking lot, without a word or a gesture, starts his car, follows my car as I drive south on Willow Street. I never even saw his face along the dance floor, where a lone guy in feathers danced too obviously, caught in some dream of himself, to the embarrassment of all six of us in the room. I should look in the rearview for the silent man's headlights, but to do so would be to replicate some scene in *Psycho.* This is nothing so fraught. I am no Marion Crane. I suppose I could pull into Cumberland Farms, get out of the car if I wanted to, buy some grapefruit juice or cigarettes. But I'm too tired to head anywhere but to the motel, where I've been holing up all weekend to write. I'm trying to finish some stories, with the idea of applying to grad school for my MFA. In the past months, I've had two stories accepted by literary magazines as well as a grant from the state arts council, but it's been hard to finish anything lately.

I turn right into the motel parking lot. Why am I not more shocked that his blinker is on, that he's making the turn past the motel sign, with the orange letters and pale green backing? Is he staying here? Of course not. Until now, my car has been the only other car in the parking lot. No self-respecting gay man would stay in Hyannis in early April when Provincetown is an hour down the road.

I get out of the car. I walk back to the room, without looking to see what's behind me. I slide the key into the lock, wiggle it, lock the door from inside. The room is silent, nothing but the taps and pings of the electric heaters. It smells of mold, but a pleasing, subtropical, Florida-vacation mold. Two drinking glasses in waxed paper sleeves sit beside an aqua plastic pitcher. All at once I feel an incredible exhaustion, and in due order, I unbuckle my pants. I kick off my shoes and socks, I pull off my sweater. I lie right down on the bed, naked but for my T-shirt, with the lights on.

The man stands at the window, with needy eyes, the droopy mustache twisted with white. I hadn't realized that there was a part in the curtains, and I am too magnetized and stunned to get up and close them. He is mouthing some words: please, let me in, please. Maybe, like me, he's someone who never does things like this. Maybe there's a wife at home, and he probably wonders what she'd think of him if she saw him in this position: watching a young stranger jerk off on the other side of the glass. I wonder what Denise would think of me, too. She doesn't think of me as a lonely person. She thinks of me as someone who is decent, loyal, sweet, which is why I shine those traits back at her. I wonder if her feelings would get cooler if she saw me right now. Maybe she'd start pulling away, calling less. The truth is she hasn't been calling so much in the last month or so, ever since she and B started ripping their kitchen apart.

I lie there watching the man's face as he watches me, until he tires of seeing what might be his own face transposed over mine—has the window become a mirror? He holds up his hand, presses it to glass, then walks back to his car. I pull the curtains closed. His handprint still smudges the pane. The car engine catches, and after a minute, I can picture the headlights drawing away.

2010 | The pond in the backyard of the Springs house is skimmed over with ice. On top of that ice is a coating of snow that hasn't melted in weeks. The snow hasn't really stopped since a few days before Christmas, and it bewilders me that anything could still be alive down there. But many things live here that aren't supposed to live in this climate: the fig tree, the crepe myrtle, the needle palm by the door of my study.

Just where the pump flows back into the water, there's an opening in the ice. What must it be like to look up through that opening, no wider than a foot or two? The smaller, younger fish draw to it, their mouths hitting the moving, wet surface as if they're gorging on oxygen. Or maybe it's nothing as extreme as all that. They're curious. They want to see what's up there, on the other side: the sky with its rushing clouds, the sun, the geese that fly overhead in groups of four. They want to see people.

But the older fish seem to think there isn't any value in looking through that window. The world is cold and deep in these months, and they know energy needs to be conserved. They do what they can to turn away from that aperture, to abide the darkness above their heads. They know how tired they can get. They don't need to know what they can't have. They've seen light too often only to have it taken away again and again. For what is its purpose if only to show them what they don't have? So they cradle near the bottom, in a mush of soft leaves, while the young ones keep tossing themselves up at that window above. They say, give us light. We want to see you.

1986 | Denise sends the revision to Iris. She tries to busy herself with all the chores she's put off during these hectic months: putting up bookshelves, rearranging those bookshelves. She thinks about the next book and how she might arrange it. Maybe she'll finally write the book based on her ex-husband's colleague, Otto Krupp, the high school math teacher who stabbed the biology teacher forty-one times until she stopped screaming and fighting him off. But when she sits down to write, she can't look at the screen without leaping up from her seat. Instantly she starts waxing the surface of her desk, and when she's finished with that, she pulls the books down from one of those bookshelves and starts the tedious but involving work of re-arranging them once again.

It's not that she doesn't like what she's written, but the doubts spread. If she'd held on to the book for a few more days, she could have made it a better book. She fears the news isn't going to be good. She tries to list all the things that Iris might hate about it: Emily's capacity to be wounded, Emily's capacity to fall in love with people who manipulate her, betray her, leave her behind. Is Iris even think-ing about the book, Denise wonders, or is she thinking about Denise, or more likely, a quality Iris doesn't like about herself? She wonders whether she's prepared to write this book one more time—or many more times. She thinks about that question as she beats pillows, does five loads of laundry, anything to resist the impulse to lie down on the couch, stare at the wall, and smoke half a pack.

Then Iris's phone call comes. The voice on the other end is neutral, supportive, relaxed. You've done it, Iris says, with a tired-ness that suggests *she's* been up night after night with the book. She talks about possible edits: the opening, the ending, the passages from Emily's mother's perspective. We can't help but wonder whether Iris's tiredness is disappointment, or more troubling than that, a hunch she can't even articulate at her desk, twenty stories above the Manhattan sidewalk, where the people below walk three times faster than they walk in Philadelphia. No, it is far too early to think dark things. Iris might not have her *Good Deeds*, but she certainly has a book she can work with.

Wave

2010 | In the past month: an earthquake in Haiti, an earthquake in Chile. Three debilitating northeastern snowstorms. A total of sixty inches of snow in Central Park, the snowiest winter on record. What can we look forward to next? Another earthquake or superstorm? The world has always been in some sort of frenzy, but in the past several decades we've fucked up the world. We've cut down the trees; we've burned too much oil; we've put ourselves in a position where we're using more electricity than ever. How many tools are in our hands right now, iPad, iPod, iPhone?

The TV is soundless as I write this morning. I peek out the corner of my eye and go back to my laptop screen. I believe I am waiting for tsunami waves to crush the docks and benches of Hawaii, the little buildings around the harbor. Raw destruction: that's what we want. A man running down a green stretch of lawn, a smaller man grabbing a tree trunk as water swings his legs up to the surface.

But a wave does not come without warning, as an earthquake does. Neruda: "I awakened when dreamland gave way beneath / my bed." No, a wave is all height and density. We can't hope for a weather front to block it. We can't expect it to take a different course. A wave is absolute. A wave is the voice we can't hear coming; a wave is the song of fire. We watch helplessly, but greedily, as the unaware still sleep in their beds, the animal cry of the siren filling up the dawn. And then a porch light trips on.

1987 | I'm not sure how I've ended up working as a technical writer, in an office park in King of Prussia, a full hour west of Cherry Hill, but it's a relief not to stand in front of several classes of comp students, which is what Denise is doing these days. She's decided that teaching is preferable to my full-time work week, even though I tell her about taking full advantage of my job's flextime policy, about slipping down and out the back stairs without telling anyone. The truth is Denise is probably on fire in front of the classroom. I imagine her getting larger: a generous, challenging, tough, wise creature. I imagine her walking back and forth in front of her students, gesturing with her beautiful hands. She's talking about *Beowulf* or *Hamlet* or *The School for Scandal.* Certainly she knows her students are in thrall to her. She can see the glint in the eye of one young man with thick dark hair; he always sits in the back, knees spread wide apart, the back of his head pressed against the wall. She makes sure to make eye contact with him; it is good to see that hint of a smirk in the corner of his mouth, before her eyes move on to the next person.

To have such charisma and control in front of the room! Whenever I teach, I am fighting the oncoming wave. I can't even sit on the desk in front of them without feeling it on my back, the cold of it, purified from coming across a great distance at sixty miles an hour. If only those students in the chairs knew that I was never in AP English, that I hardly read books in high school, that I once got an F on a pop quiz on *A Raisin in the Sun* because I'd never even cracked the damn thing open, though we'd been talking about the play in class for two weeks.

Still, I like the people in my department. They're smart, funny. They're worldly. A motley mix, one is a former dancer, one is the former bass guitarist for a rock band. Even my boss is a former resident of the writers conference in Vermont. I'm sure this is why she hires me, as everyone's title here implies the word "former." But they make the former an entertaining place to be. Not that we don't work hard, excessively hard. There I am, writing end-user notes for Real Property and Mortgages when I've never had a home of my own. Most of the time I don't know what the hell I'm doing. One of these days I'm going to be found out, and it will be worse than any infraction related to the study of English literature.

One day, on a business trip, a prospective banking client asks, is your background in mortgages and notes? I practically weep, *no, Shakespeare!* Oh, Shakespeare: Hamlet would know what to do with a question like that. It helps to set the alarm for five every morning, pull out my legal pad, prop the legal pad on my bent legs, and write in bed for an hour. Sometimes I can't even read the sloppy penmanship when I get home that night. It looks like the penmanship of someone with a personality disorder. Still, the act of writing gives me permission to do that eight-hour day. It is a ritual, an act of stillness, of saying *here I am* to myself. No, I haven't joined the ranks of former artists, though my coworkers might not exactly be aware of that. By the end of the year I have put together two stories I'm reasonably proud of, stories about an intense, expressive mother and the disoriented son who wants to take care of her and doesn't know how to begin. One of these stories centers upon a broken Tilt-A-Whirl ride. The story itself is divided into twelve pieces. By that I mean individual moments in time are separated by white space, and by stumbling on that form, I have found a way to sound a little like me.

But one day, I've had enough. Enough of waiting in stalled traffic on the Schuylkill Expressway. Enough of behaving myself during a regime change at work, where the new CEO tells us that flextime will soon be a way of the past. No more funny postcards on our cubicle walls, no more torn T-shirts worn on the job. Dress code, work on weekends, abrupt layoffs to keep everyone on their feet. The stock market crash has knocked the company off its feet, and we've been made to think we've contributed to the mess. At least I have another place to go. At least I've already been accepted to two residencies, one in the Berkshires, the other over the border in Upstate New York. When I go in to tell Jean, my cool, sweet boss, she completely understands why I have to leave. She doesn't make me feel as if I'm letting her or anyone else down. She looks at me as if she'd even like to go along with me. No one wants the ship when the captain is already taking it down.

2010 | At some point in the tsunami coverage, I know that the disaster is not going to transpire. Perhaps it has to do with the intensity of the vocabulary: receding, discoloration. Or the tone of it, which is a shade too portentous. Rick Sanchez, for one, is so pissed off with the affable manner of the scientist he's interviewing that he yells at him. Sanchez waves his hands, demanding his guest not sound so nonchalant. Sanchez has a story he's responsible for, and he must think he'll look like a fool if there's no story to tell.

I'm simply bothered that I've organized the afternoon around the event, which has been given an estimated time of arrival, as if a jetliner is coming in to the Hilo Airport. The speed of the wave has been compared to the speed of a jetliner, and perhaps that's what I find compelling about the phenomenon. But there is that impulse in us that says, come on, wave. Come on. Slop over car and grass and shrub: come on. The inevitable, this *thing* that wants to do us in: we can't watch the spectacle of it with any distance or detachment. We can't see that this wave is not about us.

Artist Colony

1988 | I don't yet see that living in an unheated chicken coop in the Berkshires might not be the best way to spend a late winter month. Nor do I see that cleaning the bathrooms—including the toilets, with their scum and mysterious splashes—might be fairly low on the rungs of the chore ladder. I'll take shoving logs into the wood stove in the middle of the night. I'll take getting down on all fours and scrubbing the bathroom floor; no one could have known it was sky-blue beneath all that gray. But cooking is work for another animal—I'm sorry. I can barely heat up water for Red Zinger tea. And I worry all week until it is my night to help out, and when I do, I prepare the tabouli and the hummus as if I've been eating the stuff all my life.

In short, I am happy here. I am happy to wake up to the frost inside the windowpanes every morning. I am happy not to think about the coworkers, parents, or friends I've left behind. Happy, happy, happy am I in this place that is really more commune than colony, only ten people here at a time. I am so happy that I wonder if I've even called Denise. The single phone booth in the dining hall must be shared by all in the span of an hour. If I do call her, I'll only talk for five minutes, because someone will inevitably be waiting outside to call her boyfriend or art dealer. It is good for Denise not to have an outlet for her obsessions. Maybe it is good for me, too, though I miss her terribly sometimes, especially on those nights when someone's said a thoughtless thing. I can just hear her, aghast. *What a stupid thing to say.* And yet the dirty floors, the chicken coop, the woodsy meals—all that has given me permission to be someone else. I work on a very short story that takes me three full days to write. I work on another story about a curmudgeonly developer, Clem Thornton, builder of Walden Ponds (Thoreau Lane, Emerson Road, Margaret Fuller Court). And—an idea catches in my head like a piece of straw to my wool sweater—Clem's grandson, Red, is attracted to other men. Red is in charge of the story.

I look out the window toward the brushy field, but I'm careful not to look too hard. Today David, a visual artist, is cutting a path. He looks as if he's done this kind of work forever—see the tightness around his eyes and chin, his grip on the scythe. He is gay, and happily so. It isn't even an issue with him. It goes without saying that the others expect us to find each other attractive. I think about the paint-spattered black sweatshirt he wears every day, his ponytail (all of two inches), the silver hoop in his right ear. I like his style. I would like to look like him, possess his effortless cool, but he is simply not my type. My type tends toward big, stumbling lugs who don't have much truck with effortless cool. That's probably true of his type, too, which might be why we make each other nervous. Our exchanges are full of awkwardness: halting sentences, strained cheerfulness, self-conscious silences. It's always a relief to be joined by someone else whenever we are attempting to have a conversation in the dining room, or else one of us would have to run away.

I work on my story. For whatever reason, all my worries about gay content fall away. I stop thinking about how readers are going to hear it, whether they're going to think I'm Red. The story moves along its own rugged spine, and oddly, it's the plainest thing I've ever written. The descriptions aren't as quirky as my usual descriptions, the tone doesn't live in the slippery zone between the comic and the serious, and the breaks between sections seem to have disappeared. Everything is fused, written as if it happens at a single moment in time.

One night, late in the residency, I read my story at the group reading that happens once a week. The only way I can read the story is to pretend I've been reading and writing such work all my life. And I do that without stumbling or lowering my voice for emphasis even though that might have won me points. I pause after I'm finished.

Outside, on the grass, a robin makes that strange song at dusk that sounds more like a death song than a greeting. And then I look up and make sure not to walk away from the podium too fast. For a while, everyone's quiet; no one knows what to say, how to say it. And then they're talking, talking too quickly, reaching out to grab my hand, hug me longer than is comfortable, hands on the back of my damp flannel shirt. The women love it in a way that makes me grateful but red hot in the face. David, to my surprise, says kind things, better than kind things. His eyes fill up as he says them. Then he dashes into the dark to his studio out back, where he'll paint to the Smiths for the rest of the night. But the men, the two Roberts? They don't say a word, but look at me as if all the doors will open for people like me—and not them. It doesn't exactly help that the women won't let me go. Oh, they won't stop talking, these women, straight or gay, all the women the Roberts have been wanting to sneak off into bed with.

I make eye contact with the Roberts for the rest of the week. They appear to pretend that they've never heard any story from me; so be it. I expect so little from anyone that my feelings aren't hurt.

2010 | We submit to our TV screens. In Hawaii, all the schools are closed for the day, all the malls, the banks, the office buildings. Soon the water discolors a bit. The green of it goes a little ashy around the point. We look at the phenomenon the way we once might have looked at the moon when we were children, as if through determined looking we'd see new life in it. But there isn't anything new here. The water recedes some. And an hour later, the spectators on the hill in Hawaii seem to shrug all at once. They slide their phones in their pockets and purses. They get in their cars, not knowing what to do with their agitation, and drive back to their homes with it.

1988 | Denise holds her cup of coffee against her chin. Her eyes are open, but it's her listening gaze; she's never looking near me or at me. She's looking at the space just above the bowl of limes on the dining room table. She's waiting for adventure, revelation. A truck ticks on the cobblestones outside, engine off, cooling. She lights up a cigarette. I'm reading aloud from the new story, trying not to listen to myself, trying not to take in the fact that I'm not hearing her usual sounds of agreement or surprise. I've been thinking about this night ever since I've come home from the Berkshires, half with eagerness, half with dread. I do know that life cannot proceed without getting this message out. I am different in my bones and blood, as strange as that may seem, and perhaps the bodily necessity of that helps me on. I'm not as anxious as I would have expected to be. I'd be drowning tonight if I tried to pretend nothing had changed in that month away.

I should be crying, but I am not crying.

I take a sip of water. It helps that the story also feels less like me than ever. The reading at the artist colony helped me to take it one step further from myself, and now it's already another step further. Me? This story isn't about me. Perhaps that's why I can read it at Denise's long dining room table, in the new town house near the Art Museum, knowing that she's thinking about Red and Clem and the empty model homes they're walking by at dusk, the acres ahead of browning fields, unfinished streets.

"Is that you?" Denise says.

The brightness of the lamp on her face. She says it casually, though she mustn't be feeling so casual inside. I must nod or shrug.

"Well, that was a good way to do it," she says, friendly.

She smiles. She goes on to talk about what she loves about the story, as she's always done, taking special pains to treat it as if it's just any story of mine but better, truer. The lamp is still here, the tree outside the window is still here. The limes on the table, the truck. The heating system kicks on with a mathematical hush, but I feel as if I've just finished moving an entire household, a box at a time, up five flights of stairs. Then carried the whole household right back down again.

Can I lie down now? My head hurts, but it would confuse her

to let that be known. I should be relieved, but I already know it's not so simple.

Then we talk about all the usual things, her parents, my parents, the student of hers who's demanding an A over an A minus. The terrible cover they're using for her novel. We know the new cover, with its acidic palette, is more likely to attract attention, is livelier than the single sad trumpet of the previous version, but we must convince ourselves we like it every time one of us holds it at some distance across the room. We're afraid to say it's not working, afraid to say it's going to sink the book before it even gets the chance to float, because that just feels like doomsaying and there's so much to be hopeful for.

A thought must also run through our minds at some point that evening. Why had I waited so long to tell her? What did I lose by keeping myself closed for so long? The costs of bandaging, mummying myself: how long will those costs go on? They couldn't have been good for us, those costs. They will play out for years, we know it, in ways we'll never be able to predict. Of course we are already in the new house, the stronger, brighter, more modern house. It's the house everyone wants to live in. It's expensive, spacious; light cleans its rooms. But I'm already wondering about the lost house, the eerie permissions of its clutter. The rooms you could never quite make out because it was dark there. You always liked the dark.

Why can't we ever have two houses at once? Openness, hiddenness, then back again?

But at least this time is better than the last time: my mother's hysteria, my father's silence, fuming silence. And the newspaper article left for me at breakfast one morning: GAY CANCER KILLS 100. To sit there, eating my shredded wheat casually, as if the headline, folded in half with such care, were meant to be read by a stranger and not by me, someone who thought he was known and trusted by them.

I wouldn't want to live through that ever again. I won't have to live through that ever again. Denise and I will sit around the table.

We will talk more about the new cover of the novel and try to get used to it. A piece of hair falls over her eyes, and then a shadow. I never wanted to be closed to the ones I loved. I wanted to be generous, transparent, available. I fear that I've failed her, but there's also been a beginning. In a little while, it will take a little less work to walk across the room, to hold up that book cover when she asks to see it one more time.

2010 | Grief is over. By which I mean that tendency to see endings written in the things themselves: plants, houses, animals, trees, faces. That capacity to think of any face and imagine the stages of its aging, the rings beneath the eyes, the sag above and to the side. Not just its aging, but its absence. A shock in the chest every time any face is conjured up, the little girl playing with a garden hose outside the farm market, the horse running around the track, eyes alert, in the prime of his form. It wasn't exactly awful, that place. Perhaps it was beautiful to think of the loss of the body, any body, ten times an hour. Though we certainly couldn't live in that place month after month. We would exhaust ourselves, the brain turning to pencil shavings, or worse.

Grief is over; I tell myself that. It is over. I'm even tempted to say it aloud, as a charm, a dare, even if I know I might be bringing about disaster by doing such a thing. Six months after the loss of my friend, and life is a ruthless, acid thing. It can never get enough. It can never fill its mouth, its gullet. And just when you think all is balance and equipoise (see my straight posture, my neutral face? There I am, halfway across the balance beam), a hand from nowhere pushes against your back. You think you've already endured your test, just when it might only be beginning.

From "The Kitchen Table: An Honest Orgy," Denise Gess (2007)

We examined [the table] again. It was pockmarked and scratched, and initials had been carved into it. Who were "D.H." and "C.A."? What boldness or recklessness had led them to make their marks here rather than on the trunk of a tree? As I ran my hand along its surface, I was delighted to discover a smooth depression in the left corner; the palm of my hand slipped snugly into that worn section, where, I decided, many other hands must have rested, gripped, slammed, and pounded the surface while negotiating the everyday struggles of family life. Surely it would serve us as well, humble us with its simplicity, and provide the setting for forming connections. This would be the table at which I could keep an eye on my daughter and stay in touch with her and her friends. This would be the table where B (who claimed to need and love and miss sitting in the kitchen) would linger with me in the mornings before going off to work, and where we'd find each other again late at night to talk. And, given its general appearance and long history, I had faith that any human accident—spilled juice, a hot dish that might leave a mark, a harsh word spoken carelessly—would be forgiven here.

1988 | I am sitting around the table on the fourth floor of EPB, the English Philosophy Building, where I am a student in T. C. Boyle's workshop. I have been in Iowa City for all of two weeks. The voices around me dart and shatter. Perhaps I'm too busy shaping what I'm trying to say—it's never more than ten words at a time—to take in any of it. When I do find the courage to speak, I feel the pressure building inside me, the faces turning toward me. They're not used to hearing my voice, not in workshop, at least, so when I do talk, it seems to count for more than it should. After I have spoken, I'm dizzy and a little sick. I have completed my self-assignment. And *then* I can take in the words around me: *this ending is skirting manipulation, this story would benefit from a more expert attention to pacing.* Such intensity around me, in me, even when no one's talking about my work. Sometimes I wonder whether the brains beside me are going to catch on fire. The words are wielded as if by a soldering iron, both hurting and fixing the story in front of us, even though the words are often kinder, more enthusiastic than anyone would have expected.

I wonder if Denise would think that. I wonder if she would have put her application to the program in the mail, ten years back, if she'd had any glimmer of its atmosphere. In order to be in this program, I've had to forget how much she'd wanted it once. I've had to tell myself my being here does not mean her not being here. That is true, of course, but I'm not sure whether she thinks that sometimes. How do I know? Just a tone in the voice, a snag in the sentence. It hurts me to hear it, but I never let that in until long after I hang up the phone. And I never talk to her about it. I think it would tear open a chasm, and I'm afraid the words would never stop coming. The words would be too hot to hear, searing me with too much wanting, the kind of wanting that could only do damage.

Is Denise getting more and more competitive with me? It's funny that I still don't allow myself to think of that word, as if it's beneath us, the dirtiest word in our lexicon. I need to hold on to the belief that our love for each other comes first.

In spite of these worries, I do feel curiously awake and alive, not quite a thousand miles west of home, west of the ocean. Sometimes I convince myself I actually like the grain silos, the strip malls in town, the clouds growing gray on a humid day, the treacherous ice storms. Sometimes I feel so alive that I must lie down on the blue wall-to-wall carpet of my apartment and stare up at the granulated spray ceiling until I can feel the heat coming back into my toes and forehead. In an hour I will be driving with my friend Katrina to the Amana Colonies, where we will eat fried chicken, rolls, cole slaw—or more likely, Katrina will watch me eating. It seems to us that there are about ten places to visit within fifty miles of Cedar Rapids and Iowa City, and we've gone to every single one of them twice within our first few weeks.

Thank God for Katrina. Since the first day of the workshop we've been inseparable. She is piercingly intelligent, funny, a gradu-ate of Harvard, a brilliant poet. We go to Econofoods together, we go to the downtown ped mall together. With her dramatic mane of thick hair, half blond, half dark, she is a lioness. She is the kind of young woman that the camera would linger on in a party scene in Fellini's *8½*. She has a beauty mark. All the men are crazy about her; a few of the women are, too. She knows about my sexuality from the get-go, and thus the whole drama of disclosure and hiddenness does not cloud who we are for each other. We can concentrate on what we really need to do, which is to fret about the lack of sexy men in town and dance at the 620, the gay bar on the other side of the railroad tracks, every Saturday night. We are practically married in all ways but one, which is likely confusing to those outside our unit. We even have our own names for each other: I call her Helen, she calls me Troy. She's even written a poem, a great poem, about an imaginary baby, "Troy's Baby."

Is this the beginning of the end of my attachment to Denise? It is a fiery question. When I tell her about workshop parties on the phone, I probably take on the voice of an insider, of someone who's no longer in awe of this strange new world he's found himself in. When I talk about *this* visiting writer, my voice might take on the bored detachment of my most skeptical peers, who look up at the ceiling each time a well-established middle-aged writer takes to the stage to read from his latest volume of middle-aged work. Who knows what Denise thinks when she puts the phone down? Does the content of our conversations keep her up at night? Does she hear the name Katrina one more time than she can bear? Is she too jealous to let it out? Maybe she calls DyAnne or Lisa or any one of her friends, and they shake their heads and talk about the fact that I used to be a decent fellow—the old story, another person corroded by ambition, by his proximity to an in-crowd. Years later, Denise will actually say that I was impossible then, and it will scorch me. I want to say, do you know what it was like to be under such scrutiny? Do you know what it was like to feel the earth shifting beneath your feet, week by week, depending on the story you put up? It was so stressful. Don't simplify me! I'm more complicated than that! You, me—we're both more complicated. Where is your dignity? But instead I steer the conversation right over that seam in the sidewalk, and once again we are talking about the person we've been talking about, some writer whose desperate urge to be seen and known might be eating up her soul, leading her to do things she probably really doesn't want to do.

It seems odd that Denise and I might be coming apart just as I've allowed myself to be closer to her. I am certain this is not my doing, even as I am certain that Katrina is beginning to take Denise's place in my imagination. The shock is that the shift has happened in months. So quick, so clean. And yet I must feel awful for leaving behind the friend who once meant everything. The feeling is so deep in me that I can't even look at it, talk about it. If guilt had a form, it would be as thick as sludge: cold, white, spoiled, like the guts of an animal.

One day I'm inside the town bookstore with Katrina and my buddy, Chris. I watch Chris pick up Denise's book from the display. It must have arrived just now; I certainly hadn't seen it when we were in the store a few hours ago.

"Look at this," Chris says, with a little sass in his grin.

He opens the book. He gestures to the inner sleeve, the description that talks about Emily and Lizzie and the playwright who's come to live with them, their tenant. He points out the playwright's name. "Eugene Lisicky," Chris says, as if I've been keeping a secret all along. And maybe I have been keeping a secret, even though it's not the kind of thing you'd tell people. My friend used my last name for a character's name: for some reason, I am feeling a little embarrassed. Maybe I should have talked Denise out of that. It's distracting; already Chris is distracted. It's not fair to the book, which deserves not to be tied down to the names of actual people.

But maybe I'm so used to hearing judgment these days that I'm missing the awe and delight in Chris's voice. The blush goes up from my neck, my gaze falls. I smile a little. I lift my head again. A flash of pride warms my ears, my face. Then we talk about Tuesday's workshop, as Chris holds the book, shifting its weight from left hand to right. He puts it under his arm, then puts it back down on the table when it's time for him to get a bite to eat.

Katrina and I say hi to KK, who comes through the door. We say hi to Brighde, Robin, Steve, Bruce, Fritz, Nicole, Stephen, Gregor, and Elizabeth, who is wearing a particularly fetching shade of dark-red lipstick today. Elizabeth and I will become the dearest friends in the future, though we couldn't possibly know that yet. We're all standing in a clump now, but I don't stop looking at the book out of the corner of my eye. Another workshoppish type nears it; his eye hovers just to the right of it. And just when I think he's going to pick it up, he reaches for a different book, a book of subtler colors, and reads it deeply as if raw truth were alchemized on its pages. Denise's book still has the cover we were trying to get used to in the spring. And, no, it isn't right. I can see now for the first time, it isn't right. No one is ever going to pick that up. Even the book itself seems to be resisting its jacket, but that's true of all the books to the right and left of it. So many books, not enough people to read them, not even in Iowa City, the center of writing and reading, where even the fucking bus driver was once a Teaching-Writing Fellow. And the book that had loomed so large for years, the book I cared about as much as my own book? It will be sent back to the warehouse for grinding in six months. I'm still too green to imagine the pain of seeing any of my own books treated like that.

Part II

A Fire in the Road

Perhaps what we love about a friendship is that it makes us look over our shoulders, stay on our toes. We watch our words. There are never any rules to guide us, no contracts, no bloodlines, just the day after day of it. It's work, though it pretends it's painless and easy. And beneath everything: the queasy possibility that it all might end tomorrow.

Maybe your duty is to have a face-to-face with your friend. You need to say, look, what you said last night hurt. It kept me awake all night. I couldn't stop playing back the whole conversation, even after the sun came up. Maybe you didn't mean to say that you liked me best when I was crying out on the pier after I was dumped, but I didn't like it, oh, not one bit.

As for what that friend might want? Maybe she wants you to push back. Maybe she doesn't want you to do your usual, which is to skip ahead and edit out the parts you don't like. She wants you to be wholly inside the movie in order to feel close once more. To see her anew. To live in uncertainty, even if it takes everything in you not to slip out the door.

I think of the high school kids who say, "We think exactly alike." We like the same music, the same movies and books. And that beach? You like that, too? I thought I was the only one who knew that beach. How much of our initial attraction is based on that kind of thing? The desire for a twin, the need to hear an echo, but perfected. A conversation with oneself: that's it. A mirror, but with another haircut.

Well, what could be more doomed than that?

Losing a lover: you don't need to be told how hard it is. It's all you want to talk about, weep about. Friends get on your side. They say, I never liked him anyway. They tell you everything that was wrong with him: his need to be the center of attention, his judgments, his capacity to bend the truth.

But you feel alive in your weeping. You weep and weep until you're cleansed by it, stronger for it. You feel as if all the salt in you is gone. All the oil and fat, the denial. After some weeks' time, you feel lean, all planes and bone, and you think, so that's what that weight had been about all about. I hadn't been happy in years. I'd been anchoring myself, soaking up water like a piece of old rope. Then in three years you're sitting across the table from someone else, beginning all over again.

It's different with a friend. The breaking up is more diffuse, though *breakup* isn't even the right word for it. Whatever it is, it happens over time, and soon old patterns are breaking: no email in the morning, no phone call at night. A week goes by, silence. Another week, a deeper silence.

Perhaps our thinking about lost friends feels like a kind of love. Sure, it might feel like rage, but aren't rage and love part of the same water?

All friendships arrow toward it: the moment of accountability. The moment at which there's a fire in the road. Smoke roiling above the break. And you can either step around it or turn back. Or walk straight into it, after which the friendship will be a different thing.

The closer we get to someone, the more we must stand humbly before her freedom.

2004 | How to say it? Denise fails me. I'm sure I fail her. How is it that we do that to each other? How could we take a beautiful friendship to this place?

Some guesses: I publish two books just as her agent cannot seem to sell her third novel. I move to different parts of the country—to Iowa City, to Florida, to Provincetown, to Houston, to New York—as she digs deeper into Philadelphia. She makes bewildering choices in boyfriends just as I've settled down with M. I think I might be finally moving into my life while she seems to be determined to hold on to what was. She and B split up. She has fallen helplessly for the man next door. When I'm introduced to this man next door, in a crowded café in SoHo, he seems unremarkable to me, a cipher, a projection screen. I stop calling her for fear that she's going to go on and on about the man next door, who seems to be the means by which she's avoiding more serious problems, problems she could fix. I think she wants to be lovelorn—or doesn't know any other way to live. It's the feeling that's keeping her alive. She's Emma, Cathy, Anna, Mrs. Bridge, Vanessa Turin, all the heroines she's loved in books, all the heroines she's wanted to write her own version of.

We became different people, as two people do over the course of many years.

And yet, at the hospice, on the night before she died, her sister-in-law said, with wonder and mystery, you were the one person who stayed around.

We were in coastal North Carolina, where M was a visiting professor for the semester. Our dog, Arden, was quite literally on his last legs. No one was happy. We were a half hour east of the part of town where our colleagues lived, in a cold, drafty house up on stilts. It smelled of dust, mold. There was serious mold everywhere, in the heating vents; on the bathroom floor, behind the toilet; in the kitchen cabinets. But, as usual, we made the best of it. We made jokes about all the things that didn't work. We shook our heads at the theater that showed *The Last Temptation of Christ* seven times a day, from 9 a.m. on, or the poor owners of the Indian restaurant whose menu cover featured the statement: WE BELIEVE IN GOD. We drove to Southport, a little town by the water hidden inside live oaks draped with Spanish moss. We drove to Kure Beach, Carolina Beach, Topsail Beach, and even Myrtle Beach, which always seemed like a bit of a hoot, with its pine trees, pancake houses, outlet malls, and Dolly Parton's Dixie Stampede.

But the promise of Denise's visit, at the halfway point in the term, made our isolation bearable. She was scheduled to be part of a group reading at a local bookstore, and it seemed like a fun idea to combine that with a longer stay. She'd been a visiting professor at the same university three years before, and though she was cautious about coming back (the permanent position she'd applied for had gone to my friend Robert), she'd wanted to spend time with us. Now that she had a new job close to Philadelphia, the lost thing could hurt less. And maybe we just wanted to compare notes, to see how we saw the place together. What to make of all the crosses and military stickers on the car bumpers? Certainly M and I must have seemed strange to the people who came in contact with us: two tall men with shorn heads and facial hair.

So why don't I remember more of the fun we must have had during her stay? I know we walked on the beach. I see the pier getting closer and closer as we walked to the north, the underside just ten feet over our heads. Feel the shells in the tidal pools, just getting warm now, beneath our bare feet. See us driving past her former apartment in a squat wooden compound downtown, college housing, though she never described it as such: green-gray, dim, a barracks with a flat roof. See us sitting at an old-fashioned seafood restaurant near the beach with our mutual friend Sarah, where the three of us must have laughed as we ate fried seafood and cole slaw, getting used to the feel of the three of us together.

It's important to name these things. I need to say that there was delight when that visit has concentrated into two memories. I don't want to define that visit by only two memories. There is always more, isn't there? There is the life the cup can't possibly hold without spilling.

Event number 1. Sunday. We drive over to the bookstore, on the other side of the drawbridge, where Denise is to read with some other writers for a new anthology. The editor of the anthology is already standing by the display of the book. Denise walks over to him. Instantly the energy isn't friendly inside. M and I stand back, give them the chance to say their hellos. We're waved over. I'm not sure why our hello is received awkwardly by the editor. It isn't what he says, but what he doesn't. It's all in his body language: eyes averted, a weakness in the handshake. It says, I'm only interested in players. We come from different species. That is okay. We step away, as if instinct tells us there's no fellow feeling to be found around here. We stand on the other side of the store as it fills up with Denise's former students. I'm not as confused by our exclusion as I am by the spectacle of Denise working hard to impress the men, the straight men, as the five of them stand in front of the store. She's trying. She can feel all their energy moving toward her, and she's pulling it up through herself, as if she's convincing us that these guys are the people to know. These are the people who will help her. And she wants us to see how valuable she is to them. Maybe that's true, right here, now. The editor also runs the book section of a large-circulation newspaper; he has assigned reviews to Denise. He has made sure she's writing about the important writers of the moment so that her name and quote appear on the covers of the paperback edition. That is all great. I tell myself it's okay to be a spectator. Am I jealous? Maybe not so much jealous as confused. But to bear witness to the theater of power and exclusion? Well, I'd rather not be a part of that.

Event number 2. M, Denise, and I are just back from dinner at Indochine, our favorite restaurant, along with Sarah. Perhaps we have had a glass or two of wine, but nothing more than that. We're sitting in different positions in the living room, M and I on the rattan sofa, Denise and Sarah in separate chairs. The smell of mold is a little more forgiving tonight. The room feels different with four people in it, the knotty pine looks friendlier than I would have expected. We're talking about a fiction writer we all know in common. He is a kind man, but a troubled man. It's the troubled part of him that makes him both appealing and not. He's so consumed by his own problems that he can't see he isn't the giving person he thinks he is. I make an observation about a recent story of his. I say a word or two about sentiment and earnestness clouding the thinking in the story. The magazine in which it appeared just happens to be on the coffee table, and I pick it up, read a little bit of it aloud, not in my usual reading voice, but in an actory, hushed, sentimental voice. It is not my most generous moment, but my point has been made. Sarah and M shake their heads in agreement. I look up at Denise's eyes, which are wide open and watching me.

Sarah gets up to leave. We hug her good night. I tell her we'll see her in a little while and we close the door. We walk over to pick up the glasses from the coffee table. We start to turn off lamps and begin straightening up. And here everything comes undone. Linearity is not possible. Order? See what you think. This I remember: M and I sitting on the couch while Denise paces back and forth in front of us, a hunted animal. Or more likely, someone pleading her case. She's a hurricane of woundedness. Her hands are moving, incisive. She crouches in at her waist to emphasize that the story I made fun of was a good story, a great story. She is not making sense. Is not being specific, though she is certainly trying to be. Everything about her is crackling, electric: the look in her eyes, the tone of her voice. Pain whips through her body, making her more alive. She keeps defending the story, but the intensity is so extreme—it has to be about other matters. Is she just jealous of Sarah tonight? Have we mentioned too many names she doesn't know? Is she still upset about the permanent job she didn't get here, a job she pulled out of when she sensed it wasn't going to be offered to her? Does she blame Sarah for that? Maybe she pictures the three of us sitting down at some greasy spoon tomorrow, laughing about her after she boards the plane— pure paranoia. All we know is that she's a force we can't speak back to. There are no words to calm her, soothe her. She won't respond to reason. And just as quickly as the outburst started, it stops as if no body, no throat could sustain that howl for long. She's herself again, looking at some knot on the wall, trembling a little, vulnerable, shocked by the emotion she's spilled all over us.

If that emotion were water, it would be dirty, trapped in a tank until it turned dark green.

We use that time to say good night, slink past her, and secrete ourselves in the master bedroom.

"What was *that?*" M whispers, after we pull two layers of covers over ourselves. The bedroom is dark but for the yellow reflection of the porch light on the oleander.

I might be shaking. For the briefest instant I press my palms into my eyes, as if too much from outside might be leaching into them.

Across the hall: teeth brushing, water splashing on the face, water running in the sink. The shower turns on and stays on. A troubled spirit is in our house. It is pushing into us. Outside the cabbage palm threshes in the wind.

"That was crazy," M whispers. "I've never seen anything like that. Is she on medication?"

I whisper no.

"Did she drink tonight?"

"Maybe a glass or two. No more than Sarah."

"Is she having a breakdown?"

"Not that I know of. She seemed fine, perfectly fine all day."

"At dinner?"

"Yes, at dinner. She made Sarah and me laugh. She seemed to be having a happy night."

I feel awful and worked up, as if I've been responsible for bringing a dark force through the front door. It would have been bad enough to be on my own with it, but M seems to have taken Denise personally, as if the spirits of his difficult past have joined forces in her and confronted us, insulted us. (The mother of his high school

years, pointing the loaded gun at him; the father who sends back
his memoir manuscript with the words "Return to Sender" on the
envelope.) He is not happy with me, and I feel it bodily. We are not a
couple used to fighting, to living in the midst of confrontation. Calm
and equilibrium are how we get by; we are at sea when they're dis-
rupted. As for Arden? His dry nose points east, completely oblivious
to what's transpired around him. Maybe it helps to be deaf.

Is it Katrina? She's on the other side of the country, teaching,
busy with young children. Iowa? Too simple. Provincetown fellowships? Too simple. Books published? We're only talking two. Life
with a famous writer? No, no, no.

Maybe she thinks I don't like her writing. But I love it, especially when she's having fun on the page, especially when she's not
trying too hard to impress, to be literary, to sound like someone
else. Oh, there I go. A lot of her writing lately has begun to sound
like someone else, and it wouldn't hurt to write in that *Good Deeds*
voice again, if she hasn't totally lost it.

She probably thinks I think she's lost it. She's not a star
anymore—is that what she sees in my eyes? But she's been feeding
people that old story for years. At this point it's hard not to take
it as truth. "I was one of those eighties girls," she'd told Elizabeth,
with a rueful smile, when both of them happened to meet in the living room of the Provincetown house. By "eighties girls" she meant
Laurie Colwin, Renata Adler, Ann Beattie.

Anyone not now. She almost sounded delighted by the designation, as if a designation were better than none.

The next morning is just about pretending that none of last
night happened. She's clearly not going to talk about it, and I'm not
going to talk about it. She's not a decent person anymore—I've come
to that conclusion. Bitterness has changed her. I just want to get her
out and away. I'm driving her to the airport. It is the spring of Alicia
Keys. It is impossible to go to the supermarket or the gym or the
shopping mall without hearing Alicia Keys, and though we would

have sung together to the song not so long ago, we're too careful for that now. Our good-bye at the terminal is friendly. I'm sure I kiss and hug her as I always kiss and hug her. I look over her shoulder at the fenced retention basin. The grass around it is mashed and browned. We are silent about last night. Or if she does acknowledge any strangeness, it's in the breeziest fashion, but that's not what I want to hear right now. *You were a guest in our house,* I want to mutter. *You behaved horribly. What if I did the same in your house?* But where would I go from there? She turns around and walks toward the door. I press the gas pedal gently before she even makes it up the sidewalk. If she turns around to wave at me, I'll make sure I'm not around to see it.

When I get back to the house, I will burn sage. I will burn stick after stick after stick of it until even the front porch reeks.

I drive back across the drawbridge through the column of palms on either side of the causeway. A speedboat races around one of the hairpin turns of the creek. It is an old story for her, a story that has concentrated as the years have gone by: I am in the in-crowd, while she's looked over, passed by, doomed, punished, betrayed, forsaken, unseen.

It is easier to play that role than it is to believe you might have some agency. No?

Well, fuck it. I'm so sick of that antiquated story, I can't even tell you. And for a good long time after that. Fuck it. I didn't care if I ever talked to her again.

I thought I could live with that back then.

Part III

Oiled, Sooted, Smeared

2010 | After a month or so away from writing—school, grading, the usual end-of-the-term deadlines—the world is new and precarious. Tsunamis and earthquakes are practically quaint, the stuff of predictability. The volcano in Iceland disrupts air service between the United States and Europe for at least two weeks. Tourists rack up hotel bills, they walk the New York streets until their feet hurt, their heads numb with looking. Can't science take care of it? Can't the governments? These questions are at the heart of the frustration, but at least we're not scorched by the lava flow. In one photograph, the fire soars and flares over the icy mountain, while a farmer steers a tractor in the foreground. The image is so extreme and beautiful that it looks Photoshopped, or like a shot from *Close Encounters.* I don't know what's stirring about it. It certainly makes us feel alive to look at such a thing. On one hand, I think, complacency and calm in the midst of apocalypse—that's it. Of course. The metaphor for how we know ourselves now. We go on in our dailiness even as the world is blowing up in front of our eyes. But even that feels too easy, theoretical. To see a fire like that in our own backyards! How it would affect the way we move through our rooms, our kitchens, the shed out back, and even how we hang up the tools on the walls.

Somehow the Gulf of Mexico oil spill feels more personal. Perhaps by the time you read this, that disaster will have a name, as other disasters are made benign and containable by a name. The chaos of the Twin Towers becomes 9/11. The first Iraq war is Operation Desert Storm. Maybe the Gulf disaster will come to be known as Deepwater Horizon, but the corruption of it doesn't deserve such a poetic name. In the past few days, scientists speculate that the oil will enter the Loop Current, head out around the Florida Keys and up the East Coast. Some reports say North Carolina. Others say the south beaches of Nantucket. A few even say Europe, and the fact that no one has a clue sometimes feels as bad as the disaster itself. Food-related words are bandied about: mousse, chocolate, peanut butter, pancake batter, pudding, patties, melted chocolate, mole. No one of course says out loud what it really looks like: shit. Shit all over the white beaches of Alabama and the Florida Panhandle. Already a duck is becoming the poster child of the disaster. The coating on the duck is so thick that he can barely see through it. We already know that the duck is not going to survive. Maybe that oiled duck is just what we need to shake ourselves awake, just the way the shot of the napalmed Vietnamese girl shook a whole generation awake. But we are already bombarded with so much. Maybe a single image can't even have consequence anymore.

By the time you read this you'll have a better sense of things. Restoration will be under way, raw green marsh grass planted, shrimp and crab nurseries sparkling in the sunlight, and the dolphins will thrive without any memory of what had befallen their ancestors. Or what about a miraculous intervention: God reaching down into the water, soaking it up with his mighty woolen arm.

Then again, the worst might come true. One species after another falling out of the world, like pages falling out of a book that's no longer read. Everything we love oiled, sooted, smeared. Not just the things we see, but the things we can't. We'll go on as a species for a while, but after the whales and dolphins and birds are gone, we won't be able to live with ourselves.

2005 | It's been six months since Denise and I have had contact. We appear to be conducting a test: yes, it's possible to shower, to make breakfast, write emails, and read student work without thinking of you. There's a sick little thrill to the test. Maybe through abstinence we're getting ourselves back. A lightness in our step, a quickness to our thoughts.

It helps that it's a busy moment. After that semester in Wilmington, I'm teaching a graduate-level workshop at the college where I've been teaching fiction writing for years. The students are eager to talk; they speak about Flannery O'Connor, Joy Williams, and Denis Johnson with happy detachment. They love literature, love one another's work, and want to be with one another in the same room. They're kind. There's no entitlement in their voices. More important than that, their work is good, very good. Somehow this frees me up to concentrate on my own writing, and I write pages and pages of a new novel that I'm convinced is going to change everything for me.

It is time to make bigger claims for myself.

Later in October I send out a group email to announce my new email address. This triggers any number of hellos from people I wouldn't have heard from otherwise, one of whom happens to be Denise.

Question 1: Would she have written to me had I not written to her first?

Question 2: Was it annoying to get a group email from me in lieu of a personal message? After how many months of silence? Sixteen?

I write back in a matter of an hour. I don't express my annoyance with the fact that she signs her name Denise rather than with any of the nicknames we've used for each other over the years. I don't say a thing about the professional request at the heart of her letter—months and months of silence and she's asking for a favor, a letter of recommendation from M, no less. Maybe she is just holding a wet finger to the wind. She is trying to see whether I'm angry with her—does she think I have a right to be furious?—but there's a distance and hardness in her lack of particulars. When I look over my response six years later, my all-too-sprightly "must go for now, dear," it's clear I want to say everything is all right. I don't want to play the part of judging her, abandoning her. But I'm not sure I believe any of it. I wonder if my cheerfulness is its own kind of aggression: *you are a petulant child and nothing you can do will shake me.* The language in my letter runs on its own currents. It is all reconciliation, forgiveness, but I'm not sure it's real forgiveness. My language is not at all besieged by the stops, starts, and fumbling of real thought and feeling. Not a single sentence has been worried over. Not a single sentence suggests, I love you and we need to build a bridge.

But I keep coming back to *her* last lines: *Hope things are going well for you. Miss you. Love you deeply.*

That "miss you." That "deeply." You'd have to be lead to resist such things.

> *Papito,*
>
> *So good to hear from you. You sound wonderful. That's great news about the film option and I think M might be on to something re: the new book. You should truly consider such a thing.*
>
> *I long to be back at work on a novel and deeply immersed in the essay collection, but time has not allowed much of either although I have managed to start sending the new essay around. [X] just rejected it last week. Any venues you think might be possible, I'm all ears.*
>
> *I know what you mean about health insurance. I have to go for my one year post-cancer check-up. I'll always need the health insurance now. The Houston job could work out well, yes? Your take on R—— is right on the money. Although that huge endowment they received allowed them to change their name, become a "university," the reality is most of the change revolves around the engineering school. . . . I do love Ron Block, though. One of my favorite days so far were the hours*

spent devising the graduate reading list. For once, we were two writers talking about writing. I've always loved going into work. You know how much I'm energized by teaching. . . .

I forget whether or not I told you the book has definitely been optioned for film. Katie threw in another bonus payment, so as soon as the contract arrives that's a go. She'll be writing the screenplay herself.

Okay. More later. I love you to pieces. Be well.

Love,

Chiquita xoxoxo

P.S. I am dying to get up to NYC to visit . . .

There she is, there is her voice: alert and surging forward. Perhaps she's relieved that we've learned to be fluent again, to renew what we'd been. It's been too much work not to speak. Too much to keep ourselves closed off while pretending to be open and alive to the things around us.

To pieces. Dying to get up.

I write back to her. Then that's the last I'll hear from her for a very long time.

2010 | On June 12, the *New York Times* reports that BP is corralling approximately ten thousand barrels of crude a day. "The cap is capturing so much oil," the report says, "that the company [does] not have adequate equipment to process any more."

Four presumptions lay behind this report:

We've had enough bad news for the past seven weeks.

Science and technology work wonders for us. Oh, pity you doubters, you travelers stranded by the volcano. All our great myths are once again affirmed.

Narratives do have rising action and falling action, and a story, if it is to be a satisfying story, must end well and be resolved.

Apocalypse has been too much for us to handle, and now we can get back to fishing and casinos and high-rise hotels.

No mention has been made of any undersea plume. No mention of the other fact, which shows up repeatedly in other forums: to cap the well, BP has had to increase the flow of oil to twenty thousand barrels a day. I can't imagine what negotiations and transactions might have gone on to prompt the newspapers to omit that bit of news.

Maybe we should stop calling it a spill. Exact language is in order. Let's call it a hemorrhage, a hole punched in the skin of the earth. That must be why the story unsettles us. It reminds us that spilling is our most inevitable condition. How much work goes into reining ourselves in at every moment when all we want to do is spill, spill?

Spillage: foul words, foul thoughts. Sickness, the body without agency. Spillage: the world that is hungry for endings.

"It could take well into autumn—and maybe much longer—to deal with the slick spreading relentlessly across the Gulf," says the opening line of BP's latest PR release.

Maybe much longer.

No mention made of the spill off the Mexican coast in the 1970s. Forty years after the fact, tar still leaches in the estuaries. Into the mangrove, onto your skin if you put your hand in sand, water. Take your hand out and it smells like fetid soup.

2005 | One sentence comes back to me over and over and over again: "I have to go for my one year post-cancer check-up."

I wonder how I passed that by when I first read Denise's email.

It almost seems that she'd wanted me to do that. Did she assume I'd rather not know? Could she hear it in my voice when she first said there was cancer in her colon? They caught it early, she'd said. Luckily, I am going to live a long time.

Then I think, no, it's not so much that, no. She wanted me to know. Yes, I am worried about my body, but I don't want this to be my one story right now. I think about my coming out to her in that dining room so many years back. The years I held back that news simply because I didn't want my gay identity to be the single subject of me. Rather, *a* subject of me. These are two separate matters, of course, but I can understand the resistance to being interpreted through a single lens.

No, I think. It is an inverted arrogance to think she was protecting me. She probably didn't want to make it so real to herself. Couldn't you bring back cancer simply by uttering its name too much? Hard enough to get through the day, to write the check, sign the check, seal the envelope, put the stamp on the envelope, and walk to the post office. And then the next day you do it all over again.

I'm sure she knew what she was doing. Cancer as disruptive as a common cold that hung around too long. I understand that. No other way to stop the dreadful faces of concern—*are you okay?* Faces that are never really about you, but about the one who asks the question. *Tell me you are okay so I don't have to lose any more sleep.* Enough to protect dailiness, simple dailiness, which must feel like adventure after you've been through radiation. To go out for a cup of coffee: precious. To walk to a dog park. To buy the kind of dress that makes others eye you and pull you in. To start exercising again. To walk the treadmill for twenty minutes, breathing, arms swinging.

A few things I know about the months before the illness. She'd lost lots of weight, rapidly. She was working very hard to finish a nonfiction book with a looming deadline. Teaching a full-time load and trying to finish a book. Living in a new place hundreds of miles from home. Cup after cup of coffee, tapping away on her keyboard as night moved into morning. The fight inside her shaping her sentences, which are more heightened in pitch and description than anything she'd written before. Although it is a book about fire, it is also the book about a catastrophe in her, though she doesn't announce it as such. I don't know if she knew, but the book certainly did.

The incident at the beach house. Maybe she was angry at cancer, at death, and we just happened to be standing in the face of it. Here she was, returning to the place where she was sick and didn't yet know it. Impossible not to associate those streets with that strange feeling in her, a tiredness. A worry over the book, a worry over the job she was applying for. The memory of her body out of control, waking up in the middle of the night to look at her face before the bathroom mirror. The flatness of the skin and hair. The strange thing it did to the hairline. The dryness: lips, fingertips, upper arms. Her thinness.

Another thought stops me: Denise's first bout with cancer comes around the same time as my mother's breast cancer in 2002. My retreat, Denise's withdrawal, the haziness of my memory around that time.

The realization of that is enough to stop my breath.

Does a realization stop breath? Of course it can. Not complete breathing, but the pattern. Perhaps there's relief in breaking the pattern, for how else would you know you have a body, a body to lose?

Maybe Denise knew I'd already had all I could take on my mind.

High Maintenance

2010 | Reporters seem to know exactly how to piss off Joni Mitchell. Ask a provocative question, call her a *female* singer-songwriter, a folk singer, imply that her foray into jazz was a failed experiment. Talk about her career as if her best songs were "Free Man in Paris" and "Help Me," songs written and performed in the 1970s. Ask her opinion of the younger songwriters who claim her as an influence, singers who have as much in common with her as plastic does with mahogany. It is so easy to get her going: watch her face get stony, listen to her voice get hard. It must be part of the assignment: Ask her anything you want, but you must ask this offensive thing. Ask this, and the article will be posted and retweeted all over the world.

Which is true of the article I'm looking at today, in which she calls Bob Dylan a plagiarist. She loves Bob Dylan; she's indebted to him for the long lines in *Hejira* and *Don Juan's Reckless Daughter,* but the interviewer likely hasn't done his homework. If he has, he chooses not to mention the influence. The pronouncement is just too choice, too ludicrous.

I wonder if Joni means what she says. Maybe so, maybe not. Both are true at once. She's upset that, because of her gender, she's never going to be called the greatest American songwriter of her generation, regardless of her innovations. The reporter, most likely a man, probably has ideas of his own: She isn't nurturing, isn't compliant. She's thorny. And what could be better than to watch a woman, an accomplished woman, take herself down in front of people?

Maybe at a certain point, after she's had a night to think it over, she feels confused about that outbreak. She can tell that the rage reads as if it's aimed at her audience. She must think, *is that what I'll* be remembered for? *Not my guitar tunings, not my collaborations with Charlie Mingus or Jaco Pastorius, but for my temper.* But then again there is so much to be angry about, so much wrong in the world, the barbarism of the music industry, which she calls a cesspool.

I put on *Shine*, the most recent album, an album I listen to more out of loyalty than love. Plenty of people who call themselves fans won't even touch music like this, with its songs about oil, mining, capitalism going awry. It is the child with the glowing eyes, the child that isn't quite right, whose head got whacked by the seesaw. At the same time, this is music for a world on the brink, brought about by its own wanting, its greed. *Strange birds of appetite.* Today the oil, if we're to believe what we read, is washing up on the shores of Dauphin Island, Alabama. The waves are actually the color of New England cider, thick, with clots of darkness in them.

High maintenance. I think about how that phrase was once bandied about a few years back, as if a loved one—a child, a girlfriend, a friend—should be a co-op with low monthly charges. A room we could live in, without giving too much back. Turn up the lights, turn high the heat.

High maintenance: someone who gets hurt easily, someone who needs special care, who can't go for two hours without blowing up, or sulking in wounded silence. And God help you if you should get in her way. She's the kind of person who can ruin your weekend just when you've packed the car to go to Maine. She'll send you to a therapist, make you lose your appetite, make you sit in a basement hall with a twelve-step group, among the glittering and wounded, who use phrases and metaphors you once felt superior to.

Go to him, sings Joni. *Be with him if you can. But be prepared to bleed.*

The friends I met in my thirties were different from Denise. They were people who didn't need to fill up the room, or express what I couldn't express for myself. We were equal partners. One didn't need to talk more, feel more than the other. It was a time when we all thought a sane life was possible. This, of course, was before 9/11, before the Bush regime, anthrax, terrorism, torture, mass incarceration, two wars, an expanded police presence, Katrina. And did we mention the Great Recession?

Maybe, at a certain point, I allowed myself to think Denise was of a different time and place. It seemed to be that she was confusing volatility with authenticity. No other reason I would have stopped finding the need to write to her about the crucial things. I was practicing, practicing for a life I believed I could live apart from her. If I could do it, she could, too. There were always people for her, not just new friends coming into her life, but family. Always family.

Denise writes to me on my birthday in July 2005. The note is straightforward, without specifics. She doesn't acknowledge that we haven't exchanged notes in eight months, but that would be ridiculous. No real friend would try to stir things up on another friend's birthday, especially if that friend was estranged.

Denise writes again on Thanksgiving afternoon, over four months later. Again, her message is cheery and fast and she doesn't say much, other than she's too busy to write. I write back instantly, as I wrote back last time, but in the writing of it, I'm shocked by what I've kept to myself.

Hello, dear,

It was great to hear from you—it's been too, too long! I've thought about you a lot lately, and have wanted to sit down and write, but there's been too much to tell. We'll have to talk on the phone soon one of these days. In the meantime, here are the headlines in no particular order. I hope this doesn't sound like an irritating form Christmas letter!

—We sold the Provincetown house last month and must move everything out by the end of December.

—We just had our kitchen redone in our apartment—a seven-month project that was really disruptive and full of drama after drama.

—I finished my new novel in September—and the last few months have been preoccupied with the disgustingly stressful project of trying to find a new agent. I just want to get this shit over with—too damn slow.

—The saddest news of all is that my mom isn't doing well health-wise. She's been losing her memory very rapidly all year—it turns out that she's been diagnosed with dementia—and she often doesn't know who any of us are. She's occasionally confused me with her dead twin. She often doesn't recognize my father, who's been her caretaker. The last few months have been awful, actually.

—Bobby, God bless him, has been able to help out with my parents. I don't think it's been an easy fall for him either. He took care of both of them after Hurricane Wilma when they lost power for a week.

—And there it is: life in sound-byte form. I'd love to see you sometime in person, so let me know the next time you're in the city. Is Austen still living in Park Slope? I hope you had a wonderful Thanksgiving—Let me know what's been up when you get the chance.

2010 | On June 12, oil-laced sargassum gets into Florida's Perdido Pass, over and through the 312,000-foot boom designed to keep out such things. Once inside, it smothers the sea grass beds and marshes, the nursery grounds for marine creatures. According to today's *Sarasota Herald Tribune*, "Rocks, grass, hermit crabs, and all manner of debris [are] coated in the big patch of rust-colored crude." We shouldn't be surprised that the boom doesn't work. They're designed for a situation with little if any current, and here the current is coming in at seven miles per hour. The materials available aren't enough to contain a spill of this magnitude. We've already moved past the initial shock; we've developed the hardness and skepticism of those whose country is at war. We *are* at war, anyway, an oilcentric war, which we do everything possible to forget. The lists of the dead are buried in the newspapers. When I am at the Detroit airport a few years back, a flag-draped casket of a dead soldier is carried ceremonially across the tarmac. The passengers inside the terminal gather at the windows, chastened by what's been kept from them, by what they've kept from themselves. Some practically put their hands to the glass as if they're trying to put a hand to the casket.

What is it, day fifty-six of the oil disaster? That sounds about right to me.

Some towns are resorting to their own methods of dealing with a particular plume. Some simply engage bulldozers to push sand around, to plug the openings between Gulf and bay. But in Orange Springs, they have their own particular solution, a plastic pipe from which a thirty-six-inch curtain holds back the flood.

"It will be contained," says President Obama. "It may take some time, and it's going to take a whole lot of effort. There is going to be damage done to the Gulf Coast." And this washed-out rhetoric from the president whom we expected so much from twenty-seven months ago. The deliverer of our people into a new age.

Over and over, reporters talk about the hardest things to capture on video and in print: the smell of the crude, which burns the eyes and the insides of the nose. It upsets the stomach until food simply doesn't taste good. It's not a substance you'd want in you.

February 17, 2006, 9:49 a.m.

Hi You,

Paul, I cannot believe how long it's been since we've spoken. Awful. How is your mom? I had a dream about

you and M the other night. Can't remember any details
except a large white marble spiral staircase and the two
of you at the top of it. The three of us were talking but I
was seeing you between the marble posts.

There've been a slew of family health problems here
since November (not me, I'm fine as is Aus) but as you
know they take up whatever remaining available time
is left.

Okay, gotta run, but be in touch just to let me know
you're both all right. Send a current phone number too.
I'll be in NYC tomorrow to visit with Austen and go to
MOMA.

Love,
Nubia

February 17, 2006, 2:12 p.m.

Hi back,

It's so astonishing to hear from you today. I just got a
call from Michael who said that my dad was admitted
to the hospital this morning. Apparently he's in serious
pain, he's been peeing blood, they put him on morphine,
and now they're running tests. The irony is that I was just
down to Florida a few days ago. My mom's in pretty bad
shape mentally. She seemed to think I was an old boy-
friend from high school, but in truth her reality is con-
stantly shifting. Sometimes she's really agitated. They've
had to put a lock on the door, because she was wandering
off, walking down six flights of stairs to the parking lot,
looking for "Mother." She's convinced that Mother lives
just across the street, and that everyone's trying to keep
her from her. My dad has been taking care of her, with
Bobby helping out some, so, God, if he goes . . .

The sad thing is that the poor guy just fell flat on his face two weeks ago while he was taking a walk. A cop driving by found him and took him to the hospital.

But M and I are fine and I'm glad to hear that you and Austen are fine.

I should be writing you in a saner frame of mind. SOON.

My dear, I must run out and do a few things to get my mind off this waiting, but it was so good to hear from you, and I do hope we get to talk to each other on the phone soon.

Love,
B xxxxx

Beneath sense lay other realities, mysteries. We don't know the half of it, and we cling to our systems and classifications as if in dread of what we can't measure. I never knew what to make of Denise's longtime infatuation with the unseen (psychics, tarot cards, the Ouija board, the portents of a dream), but I am a little more open to that today. Denise listened to whatever it was she heard: a pulse, some heat, a buzzing turned toward her. She did what she had to do, and twenty-plus months of cold war go down in a letter.

We are inside our friendship again. And her dream—of course Denise would always know when I was in trouble. I email her the next day, and then the next. In three days my father's health is better, and Denise is with me through it all, in letters, for the day in and day out of it, as I am for her. There is a sentence in my novel *The Burning House* that goes: *I couldn't unhook myself from you if I tried.* It's nothing as unlovely as all that, though. There's no other way to say it: my friend, my friend is back.

Windstorm

1966 | Marvin Gaye and Tammi Terrell look a little stagey in the video. A merry-go-round rotates behind them. Their breaths gust; it looks cold out. Tammi is in a sky-blue jacket and beret; Marvin's sport coat doesn't look heavy enough for the weather. They're singing "Ain't No Mountain High Enough," a duet that's been climbing the charts, but the performance isn't quite right yet. The voices don't actually mesh with the movements of their mouths, their arms. They're trying. They're working. They're giving the best smiles they can muster, but the two of them must know they're outside the dream of the song.

Then they seem to forget all about lip-syncing. The song swells. They're climbing higher, up the winding path into Alpine trees. Wind, rain, cold—they're leaving the elements behind. Civilizations spread out beneath them. Tammi has more swing in her gestures. Every so often she rolls her eyes, as if all this romanticism is just too much, even though she wants the dream to go on. She taps Marvin's square chin with her finger. He grins. It's too much to look at her face for long. He's glancing off to the left, not with indifference, but at a future beyond the facts. Who would want to know the facts right now? (Tammi's death of a brain tumor at twenty-four. Marvin murdered by his own father, at home. Depression, two suicide attempts, cocaine . . .) For now, Marvin's body relaxes into Tammi's, and it is just joy for the remaining seconds of the song. Not even seconds, because we're outside time. We're free-floating inside the wild sphere of what two people might be for each other.

2010 | I'm in the backyard in the house in Springs. The day has an odd turbulence about it, ever since I've picked up M from the train station the night before. Maybe I am angry with him for sleeping through his alarm clock and missing the 9 a.m. jitney. We were supposed to have lunch together, and I'd been looking forward to that lunch after a couple of intense days of writing. Instead, he will come in at five today on the busiest train of the season, the Fourth of July train, people practically standing on one another's feet, all the things people do when good manners break down. And he will be battered from it.

We walk into the house. Texts come into his phone with a frequency I find unnerving, because he never says what they are, who they're from. I wish he'd turn off the sound. Not that I expect him to tell me who it is. One thing we've tried to do in our fifteen years together is to give each other space, but the combination of secrecy and right-in-my-faceness is enough to make the hairs on my arms stand on end. I constrict from inside. His freneticism is making me frenetic, and to center myself, I go to the side yard to clean out the birdbath. There's a scum inside the dish. It's the color of raisins, but it's ugly and foul, and I don't like to think of the birds dipping their wings in that water. The week has been hot, brutally so. The air is still. It hasn't rained in so long and the birds really need to drink and clean themselves. There are no pools or puddles of standing water anywhere.

Then M comes up to me from behind. He puts his arm around me. It's part loving, part holding me in place, as if by executing that gesture, he's holding himself in place. I feel a little locked down, as if I'm being gently punished for some infraction. I wonder what I've done. "What?" he says.

"What do you mean, what?" I say. I look out at the garden. Though it's the height of summer, the plants look brown to me.

"What?" he says again, this time with more emphasis.

"Honey?" I want to turn around. It seems to me that if I could see his face just now, I wouldn't feel like falling down into his arms.

"I think you're mad at me," he says. And just the sound of those words. Oh, deep chasm: I feel the grass underneath my feet about to open up a trapdoor.

"I don't know. You're acting—you're not acting like yourself. I don't—" Full sentences are impossible. They are houses I don't have it in me to build. "What's going on? Are you seeing someone?"

It's a relief to say it, as hard as it is to say it. But it's also standing inside someone else's narrative, a TV narrative, a politician's narrative. Our relationship has always been open, but open has meant a couple of hours—and anonymity. Not an overnight stay and certainly not a boyfriend.

Some boundary is being kicked down here.

The tears burst the dam, though the tears aren't mine. They're M's. Is that what happens in any relationship, healthy or not? One cries the tears of the two. One stands ground for the both of them, but it is odd for me to be playing the tearless one. The last time I played the tearless role was at our wedding, in a salt marsh on Cape Cod, two years ago, when I read him a passage from "Song of Myself." I was astonished to see him cry in front of the minister. I'd been expecting to break down myself—that's the way I'd been imagining it in my head for months. But I spoke those words calmly as if Walt Whitman had entered me, and there I was, grateful to be released from my old role for that little while.

M continues to cry. I'm aware of the odd magnetizing force of baritone weeping—how often do we ever hear it? It has an animal pull. I imagine ears turning toward it in all the houses around us. I look over toward our neighbors' fence and instinctively pull him by the hand toward the back door.

The two of us are seated in the living room. The story is this: He has met someone. His thing with the someone has been going on, what—three meetings? They have met in the apartment in the city. They have spent the night in the city. M needs to tell me all this, because it is too much to hold it back. By coming clean about it he can begin again.

There are no plans to get rid of the someone.

And, if I'm to understand it correctly, there are no plans to get rid of me.

He says that some joy has been lost in our relationship over the past two years, though this comes as news to me. I have been relatively okay. In spite of my mother's illness and death, in spite of Denise's illness and death, I've been going forward, doing my work, teaching, getting better ever since that outbreak of shingles. What have I not been seeing? What have I not been doing? Has my own grief—the gauzy thickness of it—kept me from seeing him? Has my darkness poisoned him? The other person is forty-two. He lives in another part of Long Island. He is someone with whom he needs to have sex right now. New sex, he says, versus married sex. I get that, at least in theory. The energizing touch of another creature, a new face, a different body, a bigger chest, a furrier body, thicker hard legs, another smell, eyes of a different color. Just for that moment, I can see past myself, my own disappointment, hurt, jealousy, and rage, to the man ahead of me, the man who isn't my husband just this minute, but someone in trouble.

Maybe this guy will help him. Will take care of him in ways I can't take care of him.

Maybe this guy will help us. I have never thought we needed help, but maybe we do. I don't know anything.

And besides, we're talking about one overnight a week, right? I can do that.

I think?

Somewhere in the ghost of my imagination I think of all the figures in books and movies to whom I attach the word "accommodator." Oh, how we loathe those people, so attuned to what they think is right, to misguided notions of loyalty and attachment, that they can't even see how they're complicit. Let's think of them, let's make a list.

Am I overemphasizing my role in this so I don't have to feel the wound of it?

Is this overemphasis just another defense?

"He's such a gift to me," he says, crying and crying again as he looks at my face. "I don't know why it hurts to say that to you."

Maybe because you want it to hurt, I think. You want to slide that knife into my side with kindness on your face. But I'm in a place beyond hurting right now—the defenses are at attention. Did he think I'd crumble and shrivel? Can't he see me past the movie he's projected onto me?

"This wasn't a choice," M says, after he's recovered himself. And the conviction behind that, the openness of his face, is enough to scare me like I've never been scared before.

"You can write about this," he adds.

But I don't want this in my book! I want to cry.

2006 | Halloween has usually been a time to batten down the hatches in our New York apartment. The sidewalks crowd with people from out of town, the police barricade the streets, and for a little while, West Sixteenth Street is Bourbon Street. I suppose it is fun to have Bourbon Street out your window, but yelling and clamor are no fun unless you're with someone. M is away this year, which makes me miss last year, when we walked down the streets with black horns affixed to our heads. The night was warm, October sliding back into summertime. It was the year in which I had a long pointy beard and a photographer from the *Post* seemed to think we'd make a most interesting picture.

So no better time to get out of town, to propose a weekend with Denise. She hasn't yet seen our new second house on Fire Island, and I'm eager to have her come visit. Just the two of us.

Denise loves this idea, *loves* it. She writes me about the visit for days. She asks what to bring; she must have her coffee, she says. She must have her beans; she must have her coffee pot. Of course, I say, of course. Bring your whole wardrobe. Bring anything you want to bring.

I stand among the small crowd at the foot of the ferry dock in the October chill, watching the men in their coats—these men are older than the men of summer, homeowners rather than renters—streaming toward us. Men look past us toward other men, and they perform their greetings. It's true of us, whoever we are: we want to look popular, we want to seem loved, and we want to love back. Then there's Denise who catches sight of me as she steps off the boat. She has high heels on. (High heels on those boardwalks: Denise!) And her big grin, which she hides a bit by dipping her head, a characteristic gesture, as if she knows from experience that it could be dangerous to beam out that grin too freely.

We hug. We laugh. Suddenly no one else exists but us, and we walk down the boardwalk, past the pines, past deer, past bamboo, past the puddles in the sand of Fire Island Boulevard, as if there had never been that night in that North Carolina beach house, as if there had never been anything to get in the way of our affection and ease.

She loves the house. She loves the windows open to the holly trees and birches, the white walls, the spare furniture, the clerestories facing west. There's an extra poignancy to this time of year, just as the leaves color, the season drawing to a close. Soon the ferry schedule will dwindle to two boats a day, then only on weekends, provided Great South Bay doesn't freeze over. The water will be shut off, and if we do come out, say, on the third weekend of December, we'll have to cart the water in jugs and pee outside.

We have three days. We talk about work, as usual: the colleagues and friends who drive Denise nuts. We walk down the boardwalks and point to houses we like. Interestingly, Denise points to the single, traditional Cape Cod house among the hundreds of modern houses as her favorite, which puzzles me, but not enough to ask her about it, to make a big deal out of it. I don't know what she sees in that house that she doesn't see in the sleek wooden boxes surrounding it. We walk on the beach and look out at the cold, hard sea. I even tell her I'm going to write for two hours every day, which I do. I close the bedroom door, perch my laptop on my legs, and push a new novel just a few sentences ahead into the next scene, into time. It feels like an achievement to ask for this time alone, even though she's just a few feet on the other side of the wall. I'm still prone to her big shimmering aura, but I need some space of my own. It will be good for me, I tell her. It will be good for you. So we honor the plan. I write, while she sits curled up on her bed, in the stream of the heating vent, marking up student stories in red.

The best thing, though: we cook. Or at least I initiate the cooking. I'm not sure Denise knows how little I know about cooking, but I fake it as if my life depended on it, the way I faked typing with ten fingers rather than two, and did it instantly when I worked as a technical writer in my twenties. I cut tomatoes and peppers for the salad. She stirs the sauce on the stove. And soon our cooking is a fifty-fifty thing, and the fact that we can move, without bumping or getting in each other's way, seems like a beautiful thing. Denise sways side to side, then back and forth, holding up a hand as the music plays on the sound system. She'll talk about this night until the end of her life, not about the food we made, not exactly. That wasn't the point. The point was that we cooked together, and there was no better sign, for her at least, of two people's connection.

M writes and calls from Houston to see how we're doing. He is glad we're having a good time. I am happy to hear from him, even though the weekend is only about Denise and me. Our time, our space—we haven't had much time alone since the earliest days of our friendship. Always another boyfriend, partner, husband, friend to pull one of us away from the other.

On Sunday morning a windstorm slams up the coast. No rain, but the gusts shake the house on its posts. They whistle through the sliding glass window frames; they tear leaves from birches, holly, sassafras, shadbush. And that strange sound from outside: is that really the sound of the ocean from a block away? Denise packs—her coffee, her coffee pot, her papers, her clothes: all of it pushed inside her suitcase. She pulls the rolling suitcase down the boardwalk to the ferry; I walk beside her. We lower our heads and use the tops of our heads to push forward into that wind, to stop the sand from blowing in our eyes. A trash can lid lifts up and flies onto the boardwalk and miraculously flies back onto the can, just missing us. A doe leaps across the boardwalk as if looking for a place to cover herself. And just when we think it couldn't get any windier, it does get windier. Here we are, the two of us, walking west through what appears to be a hurricane so harsh it doesn't have moisture.

Yet no one's waiting for the boat to pull in to the dock. *All morning ferries canceled,* says a guy standing under the shelter. I can't but take in the concern in Denise's eyes, the pulling in of her lips. I must have some version of that look on my face, too. We've been so good, we've had the ideal weekend, the weekend that took back, reversed, retrieved the awful weekend in North Carolina. We've engraved a shape. We've built a story we'll want to remember, and now we're left with time on our hands, an endless coda to the song that will probably go on and on till it wears out its welcome. Imagine all those great songs from the sixties ruined by the fucking coda that will not stop.

We walk back to the house uneasily. Surely Denise will explode at any minute. She can feel it, I can feel it, and I don't see how we're going to deal with that eruption out on this desert island, even though Islip, Long Island, is in sight across the bay.

We walk back to the house. The pine boughs thrash. The backs of our necks are cold. We try to mask our disappointment from each other. We go in the house, sit in the living room. We pitch ourselves on the edge of the couch, wary of giving ourselves over to the cushions, cautious of settling in.

Three hours later the boats are running. Good-bye to our tense afternoon, good-bye to the perfect weekend that preceded it, good-bye to the dry hurricane, which has since moved eastward to Block Island and Martha's Vineyard, and in the process scrubbed the wood siding on the houses clean. We're standing in winter now. Even the air has a cleansed bite to it.

We hug each other, completely unguarded now. We look into each other's face. We kiss each other, not aiming for the cheek, as we usually do, but for the mouth. I watch her walk on the boat, which is alarmingly overcrowded, enough passengers and cargo for five boats—people standing inside, people standing shoulder to shoulder. I don't see how that ferry will make it across the choppy bay without taking on water through its openings. She waves as she steps inside, that big grin turned to me once again. Then I can't see her anymore through the fog on the windows. An hour later she sends a text. *I'm on the train back to the city. I sat between two great big guys on the boat, they were so nice to me. Thank you so much for the perfect weekend.*

Romance and Betrayal and Fucking

2010 | M is beside me, on his back, breathing in regular, steady intervals, none of the deep ragged snoring of recent weeks. I can't keep my eyes off the window—it is a completely dark window. The days are longest right now, the first birds singing at 4 a.m. I want morning, just so I can get myself out of bed. I want to move around. I want to put on my shoes and pants, before more bombs start falling through the roof. The comparison is overblown. It's inappropriate, inexact, I know that, but I suddenly understand the value of routine: the washing of the shirts and the pants, as the air raid siren rises in a wail.

Though it is dark in the room, it is startling how much I see. In an earlier life, I'd have been lying on the carpet, just like I did after the night I broke up with Eric, my ex. But I am much stronger now for these months of grief, for having worked on this book. This book, walking me through the days, Sunday through Saturday, and a full paragraph comes to me, almost unbidden as a religious text. I say it over and over, so that when I speak it to M in the morning, he might see who I am.

I've never made my map—that is the heart of what I want to say to him. I've looked at the plan handed to me; I've looked to see how I can make room inside that plan. My parents are a part of this, how they carried out their lives together. They lived as if expecting the other half to make the plan, and when there was no plan, they couldn't tell who they were to each other, where one ended and the other began.

By 7 a.m. I am out in the living room, in the butterfly chair, pretending to look at the news on my laptop, though nothing is catching my attention. M walks out into the living room, rubbing his face with one hand. We half-look at each other and say good morning. You'd never know he'd gotten a full night's sleep. He walks to the kitchen for a glass of water and the coffee pot, and I tell him we need to talk.

It is perhaps unfair to begin the day like this, but I don't know any other way. He sits calmly. I say, I cannot submit to this plan for my good, for his good. I know I say it again. I'm not sure if he's able to hear me. His eyes look a little hazy, as if he's still dreaming. At some point, I move over to the couch with him. He is behind me—am I leaning back into his bare chest? I am asking him all the questions I wasn't in right enough mind to ask the day before. I am hearing things that are the hardest things to hear, but I am taking it. But one thing gets to me, and now, unlike yesterday, I am the one sobbing and shaking. Yes, he's still holding me tight, but I feel myself moving away from him. I feel my body moving out through the open window, up through the trees, into safety and light. He even says it himself: "I feel you moving away from me." I am aware that my crying can probably be heard outside the window. I don't know why I should be concerned about the sound of my crying out the window, but there it is. Maybe it is easier to think about the neighbors and how they might be hearing what they're hearing, than it is to think about myself.

The aperture of the morning widens. Who knows how much time has passed?

Somehow our bodies have shifted on the couch. Then M's head is on my lap, my hand over his heart, his warm heart. Four lines come out of his mouth with no connection to one another. A bottoming out, a cold zone.

—*My heart is broken.*

—*I want to be buried in sand.*

As for the other two? I forget them as soon as they're spoken.

My protector. My protected. My badge. My torch. My fugitive. My furnace. My doorway. My duty. My desert. My daystar. My well. My harbor. My wave. My promontory. My marshland. My dune. My plainsong. My psalm. My fascicle. My dictionary. My archive. My tower. My giant. My thunderclap. My spine. My rivering. My sprawl. My signet. My scarf. My fly-by-night. My bankruptcy. My secrecy. My greening. My saltwater. My howling. My yellow room.

2006 | A month and a half after her visit to Fire Island, Denise stops at her parents' condo in Mount Laurel after teaching. It's their usual night for dinner. Maybe Denise has picked up some peppers for a salad from Wegmans, some cherry tomatoes. She has a hunch. She can feel it as she walks up the sidewalk, looks up at the knot in the wood siding. She can feel it even before she slips the key in the lock. Was that pot of flowers there the last time she was here? And on the other side of the door: her stunned mother, too stunned yet for weeping. Only dry sounds come out. Her father in the bathroom—a heart attack, a CVA. No surprise, her father has not been well in years, and yet it is always a surprise when a father dies. Immediately Denise springs forward, she does all the things she was taught in nursing school all those years ago. She feels for his pulse, puts a hand to his head. Later they'll find out that he couldn't have been gone more than five minutes.

The email Denise sends later that night is crisp and austere, no embellishment, a state-of-shock note.

A pact is sealed between us. The time is here, the time we've been afraid of all our lives, our parents passing out of the world, and we don't know what's next. Will it be my father, falling facedown on the sidewalk as tourist traffic passes him by? My mother, walking down six flights of stairs out the door into oncoming cars, thinking Mother is on the other side of the road? Or Denise's mother, still vital, funny, worried, and beautiful after all these years? Of course it has always been the work of children to lead their parents out of this world, but we don't know whether we'll do it well or not. Our loved ones: will they suffer in our stead—who can say? We can go through all the requisite rituals. We can say all the right things, but there's the furious child inside us that says parents aren't supposed to die. Parents are supposed to take care of us, they're supposed to be there for us. They're supposed to be teaching us how to ride our bikes, to finish our math homework. They are not supposed to be leaving us behind to this cold, indifferent world.

I take the train down to Philadelphia after the intensity around the funeral settles. Once I step into her apartment, we make little mention of what she's been through, the family tensions, the compromises, the confusions. Those matters will not be the subject of our day. Instead, we eat dark toast with blackberry preserves. Instead, we drink coffee. We talk and we laugh. Then we head to Macy's in order to redeem a gift card. But before we go to Macy's we walk down Walnut and Chestnut; we wander through Diesel and West Elm. We could not care less about buying what's on the display, the sleek sofas with putty-colored cushions, the raw denim folded on display tables. We're making everyday life happen again, which feels like no small thing given the past few weeks.

I walk through an entire day with her. At one point, while she's picking up and trying on shoes, she stops as if she is looking at a door just beyond the dressing room curtain. One of her eyes fills up just a bit. Then she puts the shoe back down, turns to look me in the face, and asks in the plainest voice if I'd like to have lunch.

2010 | Braunwyn is taking me to Cape May.

One gift of the past few months is my friendship with the woman I'll call Braunwyn. Braunwyn is a fiction writer whose work I've known and admired a long time. She teaches at the school where I've been a visiting writer. She grew up on the Main Line, across the river from Cherry Hill. Her husband's relatives live in Cherry Hill. Philadelphia, Cape May—that is our glue. It seems almost uncanny that she is the same age as Denise. She's light, where Denise was dark. She comes from a wealthy family. Like me, she likes to talk and laugh, to analyze people. She values closeness, so that when we spend a day together it feels as if we've stepped into a safe tight circle, where everyone outside that circle disappears.

Friendship feels a little light a word for what we are to each other. Brother and sister? That doesn't seem right, either. Boyfriend and girlfriend? Twins? In truth we are a little in love with each other, and we're able to talk about what all that might mean. Can there be love without the bodily expression of it? Can one put one's arm around another without persuasion, expectation? Where does it stop? Where should it stop? These are the kinds of questions I've never found language for before, and it is both compelling and unsettling to talk about things that have always batted around the room, never to come out from behind the furniture.

At some points I imagine Denise watching Braunwyn and me. There she is, across the room from us, in a chair, invisible, purified of envy.

At other points I wonder if she is fuming mad, kicking over the armchairs in the room next door, smashing the good lamps.

Braunwyn and I are heading down the Garden State Parkway, through the marsh of Leonardo Harbor. It is the first outpost of green, active and glistening, past the hard, chemical strip between Newark and Woodbridge. We are going to Cape May overnight because I cannot bear any more thoughts of home right now. Or more accurately, I can't bear the thought of S being in the apartment with M while I'm by myself in Springs. One of the beauties of Springs is the deep night, the spray of stars over the trees. No streetlights, few houselights, the sound of ocean carried across farmland and forest. The quiet can calm you when your nerves are jangled from too much city, all the worries about money, all the fears that you're using movement and overwork to run away from your life. But that quiet can also kill you if you let your mind wander off into it. That might have happened to the woman who killed herself in the house behind ours last Christmas Eve. Sleeping pills, a plastic bag over her head. A cop next morning comes to the front door to ask if we "saw anything."

Why? we say. There was an "incident" out back last night. And that's where the cop stops.

I believe Braunwyn and I present a curious picture to the women behind the registration desk. Two rooms, two people, a man and a woman who like each other, but two rooms. Perhaps we seem very quaint and old school, asking for separate rooms. Perhaps that is why the ladies are extra nice to us. They appear to make mistakes with the billing just so they'll get to hang out with us a little while longer. I don't think they are used to people being nice to them, and we enjoy being nice, spreading it back and forth until it feels like the four of us have eaten too much candy.

We walk the boardwalk. We stop for ice cream, which drips down the side of the cones before they're even in our hands. The summer is as hot as it's been in eleven years, and even though we're two hundred feet from the sea, we need air-conditioning. The pale-yellow Congress Hall is up ahead, and we cross Beach Drive, walk past the hydrangeas and the lavender, underneath the portico. I decide to show Braunwyn the old photograph I'd seen with M earlier this winter. It is still in the same place, along the darkish passageway between a sitting room and the main hall. If anything, the passageway looks even darker in summer than it did in winter, what with all the brilliant sun outside.

My guess is that no one has looked at this picture since M and I looked at it six months back. We point out the various characters, their postures toward one another, whether they're alone or in a group. Point out the people we're drawn to, those who might be a little full of themselves. We wonder how the picture was taken—how could any lens be so wide? Maybe it was done over time, which would explain the bleached-out strip at the center. To me it is a picture about death, about people presenting themselves in the face of death. Not that they were necessarily thinking about any of that, but the participants know this is serious business, despite the casual air. They can already imagine the faces looking back at them, interpreting them.

After some time on the porch with coffee (sex, sex: do we ever not talk about the mysteries of sex?) we're on the way back to our hotel. Just as we cross Pittsburgh Avenue, Braunwyn's shoe catches on a buckle in the pavement. Her fall happens in slow motion. It looks as if she will catch herself, and she clearly thinks she will, too, but then she hears herself say, oh no. She bangs the pavement. My initial impulse, before I give her my arm, is to radiate supreme calm, not just for the others around us, but for Braunwyn, who must feel vulnerable and embarrassed. As if the worst thing in the world were to be embarrassed, on an early summer night, in Cape May.

I can't say what my outward actions are, but there are people around, and I know I must build a protective bubble around us to keep those people away. Braunwyn is standing, and we are look-ing at her hand, which looks scraped and torn, but isn't swollen—at least not yet.

We take our first tentative steps to the motel when a woman calls out behind us. The voice has an intensity that you don't hear much of in public anymore. "Sir, sir!" the voice cries.

I turn. It is me who is being summoned. "She hit her head," she says. "Do you know that?"

I turn to Braunwyn. "Did you hit your head?"

That woman—the *certainty* of her—unmoors us. "I don't think so," Braunwyn says.

The woman frowns. "If she behaves strangely in the middle of the night," she says, "you get her to an emergency room."

"Of course," I say, and then we walk on.

But what if we're not sleeping in the same room? I want to say.

We look at each other, worried, as if Braunwyn might fall again at any time, if not now, then sometime in the middle of the night when she's by herself. Might she just go to bed, look at the clock on the nightstand, and that could be the last thing she'd see?

The heat has dulled my good sense. One minute I think we should drive up to the emergency room in Cape May Court House and then I think not. I keep glancing at Braunwyn, checking for the half-closed eyes, the open mouth, the confused expression. I keep wondering whether my lack of decisiveness about this matter tells me what I'd rather not know about myself: if I act as if there is no problem, the problem, if there is a problem, will simply go away.

Are you okay? This becomes my refrain for the rest of the night. "I think so," Braunwyn says, tensing up her face every time she answers. I don't like this tensing up of her face, but I can't tell her that. I say good night to her in the elevator and try to hold back the suspicion that I am doing the wrong thing. I stand outside the closed doors of the elevator, stare down at a wine stain in the carpet, before I go on to my own room, which happens to be right beneath hers.

I wake up in the middle of the night. I think I hear water running upstairs, and I breathe in and out through my nose. Not dead yet, I say to myself.

I'm up at six the next morning, maybe even a little earlier. It is already light outside. I'm too bewildered to turn on my laptop, so I grab for my phone to see several texts showing up in its window. Four from Braunwyn, one from M.

From Braunwyn: *Porpoises.*

Dozens of them, playing, breaching.

Honey, come down to the beach and see.

From M? A chipper hello, and a note to let me know that he and S are headed out to the Springs. And when do I plan to get in? To the city, he means. Which must mean they want to be out of there before I arrive.

The public bathrooms are out by the beach. I'm standing beside the building waiting for Braunwyn to walk up. And then she's walking toward me, her face transformed. She is not just the one self in front of me, but all of her selves, simultaneously. Her face shines, her green eyes suffused with light. Everything that's unique about her is shining in those eyes: humor, wryness, intelligence, vulnerability.

Those eyes say we will be all right, all of us.

"You look like you're in a state of shock," she says. Her voice suggests that she's in a state of shock, too, but maybe this morning shock is not such a bad place to be.

I look back with a shrug. "Can we still see the porpoises?" I look past her toward the dune grass, the beach, the water. The sky overhead is already matted with hot-weather clouds.

"We missed them," Braunwyn says. "They're already headed up toward Wildwood."

I nod. That's okay, honestly. It's enough to know that she saw them, enough to be swept by the story. I hold on to the image of them breaching and playing as they look back to shore.

Mystery Beast

2007 | Denise and I look out at the twenty grad students assembled in front of us. We're at the head of the classroom, seated behind a table. Though we're supposed to be co-teaching the class, it feels more like we're co-hosting a television program, and the students look back at us, probably less interested in what we have to say about their stories than in watching two old friends building on each other's sentences, mirroring each other's gestures. I don't know if I'm using my hands as much as Denise is, but I'm aware of using them more than I usually do, chopping the air, emphasizing words, points.

We're at the university in New Jersey where Denise teaches English and creative writing. I don't know how she manages her schedule. Two days a week she arrives on campus at nine in the morning only to finish her teaching at nine that night. One of her many responsibilities is to run the Visiting Writers' series, and that's why I'm here. For three separate sessions during the spring term I come down to her South Jersey campus, where I teach a workshop, lead a craft class, give a reading, meet students and faculty. The series is funded by an Atlantic City casino that needs as many community service credits as it can get, and I very much enjoy referring to myself as the Major-Atlantic-City-Casino Visiting Writer that year.

The amazing thing is that we have fun. None of what we do feels like work, though we're working hard together, listening, reading, paying attention, bouncing ideas off each other. None of that old competitiveness is in the air; neither of us is cutting off the other's words or trying to outglow the other. Our work is not about us, our personalities. We're speaking of words, the shapes and sounds they make. It is good to travel to that deep place together, to be enclosed and held by it.

At some point during one of my visits I have a hard time finishing one of my sentences. I start the sentence again and I still can't complete it to my satisfaction. The students' faces blur a bit, and— God, it's hot in the room. I'm aware of sitting forward in my chair, the back of my shirt sticking to the wood. I'm not exactly ill, but I'm not exactly in my skin either. Or I'm so much in my skin that I can't help but be all about my body, trying to listen to what it wants, but I don't know what that might be.

"I think I might be getting sick," I say casually to the class.

"You're not getting sick, honey," Denise says, with her characteristic grin. "I know exactly when you're getting sick."

"I felt fine a minute ago, and right now? Like—why couldn't I find that word a minute ago? The simplest word. What do you think, guys?" I look out at the students, who are too respectful of Mr. Visiting Writer to kid with him.

We talk about story number 2. I think I am making sense; I think I am saying useful things about structure, but the minute hand of the clock is moving so slowly, and the heat from the register is relentlessly rising, drying, dehydrating. The last time I was on campus my workload felt mysteriously light; this time I am carrying cinder blocks on my back. I see the woman by the window shifting in her seat—sure, she feels hot, too—until I realize that the person who's really hot is Denise, whose forehead is now shining with moisture.

"You can't be sick," I say to her flatly.

"Why can't I be sick? I have every right to be sick. What, you think you're the only one who can be sick?"

"This is codependent!" I cry.

"It is!" And we are both laughing like total idiots, lost in our own zone, fenced off from the students, who look at us, perplexed. They can't tell whether they should distrust us or be amused, or reach into their pockets to give us some cold medicine. Frankly, I don't know what I'd think of us if *I* were in their seats.

I take the train back to Manhattan in the morning. Indeed, we both have the flu; the sudden onset of symptoms explains that. But my flu sends me to the couch for a week and a half. Denise is out of commission for four.

2010 | Part telenovela, part Almodóvar, part French farce, part *Real Housewives of New Jersey*. I'm thinking of all the inevitable comparisons as I look out the windows of the Long Island Railroad car, past Patchogue, past Mastic-Shirley, past the scrubby Pine Barrens that remind me of the landscape where I grew up. I'm on the 7:40 Sunday morning train to Amagansett. At some point late last night I decided to come out to the Springs house, not exactly unannounced, but with—an hour's or so warning. I am too worn out and confused to make anything like a scene. I know I will not make a scene, the way I made a scene at a club in Provincetown, so many years back, when I saw Eric, my ex, with another man out on the dance floor. I simply want to know who's spending time with my beloved, in my bed, at my seat at the table—all that. I've configured him as some kind of ogre in my head, and I need to see that he isn't that. And maybe I will see past myself—the self that thinks of himself as harmed—and see that maybe S isn't such a bad guy.

Somewhere past Hampton Bays I text M to say that I'll be coming in on the 10:40 train to pick up my checkbook and some clothes. Could I be picked up? I also mention that I'm looking forward to meeting S.

I do need my checkbook and some clothes, but I'm unsettled by letting out this fuck-what-may self, the side of me I've pushed down deep for way too long. What energy is about to be released into the world? I want it to be destructive. I don't want it to be destructive, even though I imagine the pines out the moving train window burning to a crisp with the sparks of me.

M texts back to say that he will be at the station to pick me up. He says what he says without a tinge of anger.

The train stops. The doors slide apart. And there he is in the parking lot, standing behind the car, standing a little behind S. I walk in their direction, trying to keep a neutral expression on my face just as they're probably trying to look neutral. S isn't the ogre I'd expected him to be but a compact man with shaved head and a weight lifter's chest and shoulders. He looks like the kind of guy who would be right at home at the Black Party or the Pines Party. He has an electricity about him, a jitteriness, an intensity in the gaze.

M tries to hug me, and though I don't exactly push him away, I don't open my arms to him either—how could I? I picture myself leaning into him slightly, but I don't know exactly what I do. We are strangers all of a sudden, and it's worse because there's someone there to see it. S refuses to look at me after I shake his hand. I can't imagine him engaging in my pleasantries. He looks off toward the other side of the railroad tracks, chin raised, hard, aloof.

S decides that it would be best for him to wait at the train station as M takes me back to the house. The plan? M will let me off at the house to gather my things, while he drives S to Bay Shore, an hour and a half west.

My unexpected arrival has stirred up stale air. Do I really want to share a car with M and S? Probably not. I think I saw all I needed to see. No one is hiding anymore. S is real to me, I am real to S, and maybe that's all I can hope for right now.

M makes the turn over the railroad tracks, past the fairways of the golf course. Soon we're heading through the tunnel of trees. The woods are so cool and dark this time of year, you'd never know a sun was burning overhead. M is angry with me, but all that seems to dissipate when I say that it was good to meet S. There was a person there. I think I am telling the truth, at least for that moment, and I think I can say that purely without trying to get something from it, to prompt an outcome from it. I am just trying to make it through the minutes.

We talk a little before M leaves. I spend an hour gathering what I think I'll need: this shirt, that shirt, this book, my phone charger, a bottle of sunscreen I bought in St. Petersburg a few months back.

Once I do that, I start cleaning up the place. Not that it's exactly untidy, but washing the dishes, vacuuming, wiping down the bathroom sink—all of it's a way of saying that this is my house, too.

After an hour, I'm sitting on the edge of the bed, staring at the cabinet in the room, with its stripped finish, just enough of the old white paint left behind to tell you it was there. I could leave this all behind, I say to myself. I close my eyes, then look at the cabinet again. *I could leave this all behind*, I say again, aloud this time. The cabinet looks even more intricate, the whorls in the finish more compelling now that the sun is shining on the floor. The clock ticks in the next room. Then—because instincts now tell me S might not be such a good guy—I take my tax records, Social Security card, and birth certificate, push them inside a padded envelope, and hide them deep in my half of the closet.

Why am I not fighting for my beloved, my life?

Maybe after my mother's death and Denise's death, I think I deserve more loss. Loss can corrupt your thinking. Loss can trick you into believing bad things happen because you must be a bad person. Loss—too much of it at once—is sinister that way.

What the fuck is wrong with me? I ought to be punching holes in the walls, tearing out tufts of insulation, kicking chairs over.

Elizabeth Bishop: "The art of losing isn't hard to master."

My friend James: "Gay men don't get angry. They just get sad."

As for what I cannot give up?

Talking about each other's writing.

The excitement of a new poem. The pride of being called "first reader." Giving advice on an image, a line, a line break, an ending. Telling him: you should write a poem about that.

Going out to our favorite pizza restaurant where we order pizzas with artichokes, sun-dried tomatoes, kalamata olives.

Going to literary events, where if I happen to look over my shoulder I catch someone looking at us, with sweetness.

Reading together, in those moments before we fall asleep: *Jane Eyre.* He takes a chapter, I take a chapter.

Taking long trips in the car with him. Trying to wake him up when he falls asleep in the passenger's seat, if only because I don't want him to miss anything.

His hand reaching for mine when I'm not expecting it.

His face when he walks through the door, after a few nights away. His happiness to see me. My happiness to see him.

Missing him when he's away.

Getting up earlier than he gets up in the morning. That hour to myself. Then his walk into the living room. The "good morning."

The dishes he makes: squash, omelets, polenta with tomato sauce.

Years of shared references. Who else would put up with my imitations, my funny voices?

The way he rubs my foot when we're sitting side by side on the sofa, watching a movie.

Walking down a forest trail, or on the beach. Realizing our pace is in sync.

Being mistaken for brothers, even though I pretend I don't like it. Same height, same size thirteen shoe.

Unexpectedly bumping into each other in the city when we're out doing our separate errands. Having a spontaneous lunch at Westville or the Dish. The New Venus, which we always call the New Penis.

The long, involved conversations about the people we have in common.

Trying to make him laugh and feeling so good when he does break out in a laugh.

His love for animals, gardening.

Waking up to his body next to mine, even if he's snoring and it's too sweaty and hot under the covers to hold him.

Who will I be if I have to leave him behind? I have nothing: no house, no furniture, no permanent job, just a couple thousand dollars in the bank.

I might as well be twenty-three years old again.

All those fans and readers—will they leave me behind, too?

2010 | I can't tell whether the wall hanging in my therapist's waiting room is awful or beautiful or some combination of both. Whatever you think of it, you can't ignore it. The piece demands a reaction every time you're sitting in front of it, as there's nothing else in that white waiting room, just a couch, a magazine rack, two noise machines, one white, one beige, whirring at top speed, and that wall hanging, which bears a figurative relationship to the bark of a tree. But there are holes in this bark, and are those holes wounds or openings to what lies beyond—or both?

Our first session practically creates itself. So much story to tell that it's time to stop just as I'm getting going. I am relieved that J is someone I can get along with. I can laugh at myself, I can hold his gaze without looking away, I can talk about God and sex, the hardest things, without fear, and he has the look of someone who's always present, always interested. He makes me feel smarter than I am. He makes me think he won't be easy on me, which is just what I want. I want to push, probe. I want to be tripped awake by a connection I've never made. He takes but one note during this session. He records the fact that my best friend died a little less than a year ago. I think about asking him why he wrote that down, but I will bring that up another time when we are a little less involved with getting the facts down.

After my session, I take the train down to Asbury Park, where I meet my brother Michael and his family, who are up from Baltimore for a few days. My father, to my surprise, is with them. They don't know how relieved I am to see them up ahead on Cookman Avenue, as I walk toward downtown from the train station. I already know this will be a good day. So many good days lately, all of which have involved the sea. Maybe it is simply the horizon line that helps me relax, the sense of perspective that opens up the mind. Or all that movement, the active sea: the opposite of stasis. It might be what we can't see, all that hidden life, crawling, shredding, floating, flying, one thing eating another thing—all these things and more, not to mention the wonderful salt smell, the ions released into the air, energizing not just the people, but the plants and birds and insects.

In a little while the five of us sit at an outdoor café on the boardwalk, the same place Braunwyn had taken me not two weeks before. The lunch is good. Our talk is easy. We're waiting for the check to arrive when a pigeon steps up to the table. He is an especially handsome pigeon, which makes me wonder why humans often treat pigeons like crap, carriers of filth and mites and disease. Jordan, my eleven-year-old niece, stands, stomps at the pigeon. I say, *Jordan, don't.* I'm startled that these words have come out of my mouth. When have I last said "no," "stop it," or "enough" to anyone, much less to my niece? And for a moment time swells as if I slip into a slow-motion movie of myself. I watch myself and see myself shrink to a focused bead of light.

But once I say no, Jordan looks. I look. We talk about the pigeon. We talk about the iridescent green of his throat, the violet shield around that patch, the rich red feet, bright as cinnamon chewing gum. We take note of the bands around his feet (feet? do pigeons even have feet?) and then the waitress comes out to say, *That's Walter, he's a homing pigeon. He's made his home here. Isn't he beautiful?* And all eyes turn to Walter, who steps not one inch from my foot, unafraid. He puts his beak down to a board, raises his head, puts his beak down again. I don't think I'm lying when I say just for that moment Walter turns to light.

At some point during the next day, Braunwyn asks me, "What do you want of a relationship? What excites you?"

It's a bit of a shock that I'm mute in the face of that question.

2010 | I can't exactly say what drives me to church one Saturday. Well, maybe I can, but of all the things I could do to find solace, it might not be the wisest choice. I've always been drawn to the liturgy—in my teens and twenties I even wrote and published church music—in spite of my exasperation with the hierarchy. I haven't gone to church by myself since my twenties, and as I walk inside and slip into a pew, I think, *okay, I'm home.* Whenever I'm with someone else, say, for midnight mass or a funeral, I usually feel some inexplicable loss, a loss I can't quite explain. But not this time. Maybe it helps that the church is a progressive church, many gay and lesbian parishioners, people of all ages and nationalities. Think of it as a Unitarian church, but with communion.

I'm usually not so big on homilies. I usually think of that as the time when the presider makes meaningless sounds in order to fill up some space: time to look at the song sheet. But today is different. The priest is talking about hospitality—what does it mean to welcome the people we love? I'm thinking about that, my arms outstretched on the back of the pew, when a phrase of his jumps out at me. *The closer we get to someone, the more we must stand humbly before his freedom.* I am riveted. He says it once more, as if he wants it to sink in: *The closer we get to someone, the more we must stand humbly before his freedom.* What on earth could such a thing mean?

Later that night M tells me about a white dog showing up at a friend's house. The friend looked at the dog's tags; the address was three miles away, all the way on the other side of town. There had been fireworks that night, extravagant fireworks, and it was likely that the dog had run across woods, marshes, highways to get to the friend's house. The friend looked out the door and saw what she thought was a white deer. But it wasn't any white deer. It was a dog, a wet white dog, who walked right into her living room and dining room, muddy paws and all. The dog looked around a bit, submitted to the friend's petting, then slumped, turned on his side, and fell asleep.

The friend called the numbers on the dog's tags. No one answered at the numbers. The friend left a message, and when she didn't hear back after a while, she started to get suspicious. Maybe the dog was hers, the mystery beast coming up the street in the dark, out of the briars, the woods.

The next day the phone rang. A terse, gruff boy on the line, and the story comes darker, clearer. The dog's human, his protector, his mother, drowned in the pool the night before. Did the dog see it happen? Did the dog jump in the water after her, try to rescue her? Was it a suicide, a heart attack, a slip off the side while she was heading back into the house with an armful of dry clothes? The friend didn't feel she had the right to such questions, but she did ask the boy—the woman's daughter's boyfriend—if he'd be willing to let the dog stay with her for a while. "He seems so comfortable here," she said. And the boy agreed to that, if reluctantly. And who could blame the friend if she started to make plans, if she thought about driving to the store for dog food. Life with the white dog, the white deer—impossible not to be relieved that she had a reason to keep herself from going so many places. A root in her midst. Finally, after so much running around.

I suppose I don't need to say that the family wanted the dog back the next day. Or say that the friend was inconsolable, as the dog jumped in the back of the family's car, so grateful to be back with his familiars. Of course his mother wouldn't be there at the house when he jumped out of the car, but he didn't know that yet. And all the losses of the friend rose up before her like ghosts turning to flesh, needing to be dealt with.

2008 | I write, but my messages aren't answered. I call, but voice mails aren't returned. I know, of course, that Denise is dealing with bigger things than my need to know about her health. I have the beginning of the school term to occupy myself with anyway. Maybe I am a better teacher for fully occupying myself. The students write good work, not just good sentences, but work they give themselves over to. We talk plenty about David Foster Wallace, whose suicide hovers around the edges of our conversations. We talk about a statement of his that I put on a worksheet: "The new rebels might be artists willing to risk the yawn, the rolled eyes, the cool smile, the nudged ribs, the parody of gifted ironists, the 'Oh, how *banal*.' To risk accusations of sentimentality, melodrama. Of overcredulity. Of softness." We finish one class by reading a passage from *Brief Interviews with Hideous Men,* and we talk for a long time about the exactness of its descriptions, its vulnerability and wit, its refusal of the *known.*

A bleached sweet salt, a flower of chemical petals.

Also during that silence, Hurricane David hits Galveston, a place M and I know well from our years in Houston. The downtown, on the bay side of the island, is practically wiped out: saltwater, sewage, petroleum, and mud rising all the way to the second-floor level. On the ocean side, the Balinese Room, a great artifact of midcentury kitsch, half–Mob hideaway, half–Polynesian fantasy, is gone. Tiki torches, thatch roofs. Even the footings are gone, though for the next two high tides, we hear reports of its boards smashing the concrete seawall until they wash out to sea for good.

In lieu of speaking to Denise, I make her a mixtape. I spend a lot of time on the project. Every song must be right, not just the songs themselves but the order. I try dozens of versions until I find a sequence I can settle on. I print out a cover, I put it in a padded envelope, address it, take it to the Old Chelsea Station post office. I walk back down Seventh Avenue and look directly ahead, aware of other pedestrians moving to my right and left. I might as well be hurling it off the top of one of the buildings, but maybe a wind will catch it and it will sail to where it needs to be.

Wanderlust (Björk)

Trophy (Bat for Lashes)

I Defy (Joan as Police Woman)

Come Here Boy (Imogen Heap)

Our Mutual Friend (Divine Comedy)

Christobel (Joan as Police Woman)

Secret Heart (Feist)

Defrag My Heart (Britta Persson)

Vertebrae by Vertebrae (Björk)

The Sound of Failure (Flaming Lips)

Child of God (Antony and the Johnsons)

Breathe Me (Sia)

Sunset (Kate Bush)

The arc of the disc doesn't promise hope where there might be no hope; the first is about setting out, the last about an ending. The songs aren't easy. They're all volatile, explosive, expressive, melodic. They're full of harmonic surprises. There's no neutrality, no sense that romance is anything but a life-and-death proposition. They don't step lightly in the world; they're not afraid of leaving a mark on wet concrete, or turning off the listener with the force of personality. They don't want to sound like other people. They say yes and yes and yes to love, in spite of all the evidence against it: the compromises that should have never begun, the failures of communication, the disappointment surely to come, in spite of good intentions.

2010 | *No, no,* I say to M. No, not just about one thing, but about another and yet another. The anger twists his face. It is hard to see that face, as that face has never shown itself to me before. It is a complete stranger to the face that has made pancakes for breakfast, or tried to start the lawnmower on a hot day in August. That face leaves the apartment after I tell that face I love it very much, which makes me think, why did you say that? Such words only translate to: look at me, I am strong and radiant and superior in the light of your rage. I patronize. But lines need to be drawn, agreements need to be made, as much as we say we hate boundaries, borders, walls. A text comes not five minutes after he's walked out the door. *I'm sorry to leave on bad terms. Yes, arguments are good, we need to learn how to fight better.*

When he gets back, I say I want to live in the apartment for the summer; he can live in Springs. I don't want to take care of elaborate gardens, enough work for three men. It's enough for me to keep the apartment in decent shape: that is my goal. To wash every cup after it's been used for coffee. To fold every shirt once it's been taken out of the dryer. To vacuum the floors every other day, to buy sunflowers (with yellow centers, not brown) for the coffee table. I am giving myself over to guarding and keeping the apartment, and in doing that I am making it my own. I am saying, this is mine, though I don't have the money to pay for it.

The thing is this: we've ended up in a life that requires money, serious money. M makes the money, I make far less of it. M pays nearly all the bills—sometimes I pay electric, sometimes I pay maintenance. I've never liked the way this felt. For years I've tried to become better known, to write the big novel that gets big reviews, big sales, big money. I've written the novel, but no editor has made an offer on it. The rejections are appreciative, respectful. They say the writing is beautiful—and yet? "Quiet" is the word that's most often used. Quiet? I'll give them fucking quiet. No one knows how much this situation is scraping me out from inside. It's killing me. Not even M knows how much it's doing me in. To admit it to him would be to admit to weakness, a side of myself I'm ashamed of, that I think of as less than masculine. I cannot bear to think of myself as less than masculine, as subordinate, even though that hasn't stopped me from making choices, in all sorts of situations, that have inevitably put me in a subordinate position.

The big book is published finally, in a smaller, concentrated form, by an indie press. There is no big advance. By this point in time, big advances, much less advances at all, are a thing of the past. All I have is my adjunct salary. But to make more than that, as a tenure-track professor of creative writing, I'd have to move away from New York, away from M.

In my dream that night, writer number 1 is standing on the edge of a little theater, getting ready to present his one-person show on the life of Walt Whitman. The audience is dense with people I know, people from my past, old students, people from Provincetown. The show begins, and writer number 1 merely goes through the motions, as if nothing could be more honorable: to half-believe in a project and still harness the energy to walk it through. In that way, Walt Whitman is a little like the ambient noise that filters in from the sidewalks outside. But one line does leap free from the braided nest of half-believed words: *Walt Whitman is not who we thought he was but the single shining entity.*

Writer number 2, who's sitting in the front row, will have none of it. None of the glibness, none of the complacency, none of the relaxed attitude toward language itself. He sits in his chair for a little bit, trying to see if he can take any more, but he can't. He knows only hooey is ahead, so he twists to his feet midperformance and heads toward the back, if only to show the others that Walt Whitman is not the single, shining entity but fractured and dazzling. The people in the theater watch in wonder as writer number 1 steps off the stage. Writer number 2 is certain that writer number 1 comes toward him to see what's wrong, but just as writer number 2 begins to offer his apology, writer number 1 breezes by him. He walks to the exit. He slips inside the men's room, where he sprinkles white powder on the edge of the program—one sniff, two—as his mind flares, comes to life again. As for the audience: the audience is simply waiting for the show to resume. They've already grown bored and know that what they've seen has nothing much to do with Walt Whitman.

After our fight, I send some lines from "Song of Myself" to my Beloved. I'm not even sure why I rest on these lines and not others, but I can see they're about looking beyond the fence of self. And isn't the fence of self the thing we'll need to dismantle if we're going to get anywhere, if anyone's to make contact again?

> *Swiftly arose and spread around me the peace*
> > *and knowledge that pass all the argument*
> > *of the earth,*
> *And I know that the hand of God is the elderhand*
> > *of my own,*
> *And I know that the spirit of God is the brother of*
> > *my own,*
> *And that all the men ever born were also my brothers*
> > *and all the women my sisters and lovers,*
> *And that a kelson of the creation is love,*
> *And limitless are leaves stiff or drooping in the*
> > *fields,*
> *And brown ants in the little wells beneath them,*
> *And mossy scabs of the worm fence, and heaped*
> > *stones, and elder and mullen and poke-weed.*

Tree House

2008 | Denise's apartment is a little like a tree house. The living room overlooks a garden where you can hear the fountain splashing from three stories above. You wouldn't even know you were in a city unless you took in the brick walls, the jagged backs of row houses to the south. No delivery truck idling, no voices up from the sidewalk, no speeding motorcycles: we are far from New York, which I left early this morning. I think you go to a city for animation and sound; tree-tops are beside the point. But the apartment couldn't be a more tranquil space, and as a result Denise seems calmer to me than I've ever known her, in spite of the shoulder-length wig she takes off and on and off. She shakes it around with a teenage girl's giggle, in imitation of Marlo Thomas in the opening credits of *That Girl*. Maybe her face is thinner, her skin a lighter shade, but she's still there to pour me a cup of coffee, to make me a meatloaf and ketchup sandwich, to ask if I want a glass of water, to laugh and laugh and laugh.

Who knows what we talk about? We certainly don't talk about matters of life or death. Anything but cancer, *C. diff*, ports—any of those words that must be bearing too much on her. Mostly we talk about what we always talk about: books, movies, other writers, the people we know, the people we know who behave irrationally, absurdly, narcissistically—these are our concerns. Human behavior and its foibles. At one point, she says she doesn't believe in God anymore. It's not the admission that startles me, but the relief it gives her to say those words to me. Her voice betrays no anger. No spiritual journeys ahead for her, no course of miracles, and while her certainty is uncharacteristic of her, maybe her stance is a bit of a relief. She's not going to fasten herself to someone else's language. She's spent a whole life fastening herself to other people and their agendas, and maybe it's time to make a new language for herself.

I take out my phone and take a picture of her cat, who swings her head around to look at me just as I make the camera click.

I take a picture of the living room from overhead, from the half-wall of the bedroom balcony down to the white pillows, the white sofa, and the cat curling up like a question mark.

I take pictures of the two of us standing up against the green-gold Rothko print. We're side by side, Denise fitting into the crook of my arm. I thrust out my arm and snap and snap. Denise beams, her head tilted just slightly back, as if nothing could be more pleasing than sheer documentation. I, on the other hand, look at the camera with what seems to me confused intensity. Maybe my face looks intense because I'm trying to hold too much at bay, trying too hard to keep the space around us rooted and still, when I know she's already having a problem with the stairs, not just the stairs to the apartment, but the stairs to the bedroom loft. In the past few days, she's had to use a bucket in the living room because she didn't have the strength and speed to dash up the stairs to the bathroom. In another week, she won't even be able to make it up the three flights to her apartment. She'll stay inside that apartment for fourteen days straight, while others will bring her groceries, or a cheesesteak from the deli around the corner, or carry her up and down the stairs in their arms. And the apartment that had seemed like a tree house just a few days before will seem a little like a punishment, just one more thing that she'd succumbed to.

But today we walk down to the dog park in a dusty grove by the Schuylkill. I'm startled that she's able to walk. I hold out my arm; she puts her arm through the hook it makes, and we take our time. We cross Twenty-Fifth Street. We open the gate, we sit on a bench, we watch the dogs. We smell the river, part rotten, part fecund, re-mark on the warm dry breeze on our faces. We point out the schip-perke, the dachshund, the Bernese mountain dog. But the dog that really captures Denise's interest is a surprise to me: an unexpectedly athletic French bulldog, who scatters gravel and clouds of acrid dust each time he dashes for the blue rubber ball that's thrown to him. Over and over the ball is thrown to him, and each time he catches it, Denise makes a sound of delight, as if his taking it in his mouth, in air, is a wonder. The ball pops against his teeth. It almost hurts to hear it again and again, but the dog's mouth is fine. Now another dog, another French bulldog, is fighting for the ball. On a day like today, I could say that Denise might just go on making the sounds of delight for a very long time, and I'll still have my friend to talk to and laugh with. Three years from now? Four? That might just happen.

The next day I email Denise the pictures. The shots don't look as crisp as I'd like them to be—they're cell phone shots, after all. But I like the way they soften edges, soften the lines underneath our eyes, the lines in the room. I think of that softness in contrast to all the tables and machines she'd been told to lie on in the past three weeks. In that way, nothing could be better than blur, lines without a blade in them.

An hour later, these words, this email:

> *Paul, language fails because you have NO idea how very much your being here was so good for me. I swear, it had to be as powerful as the medicine they're giving me because you removed the logy, sad feeling, the exhaustion, the fear. Truly. I don't show it, but I'm scared shitless. I mean, who knew I've been working (trying to) with damn brain tumors! Teaching with them etc. So weird. That you loved me despite periods in which I believe I was not myself, too brittle, perhaps shrill, demanding, means the world to me. Means you see me, means that maybe something clear/true remains. I'm such a fucking great fake—at hiding pain, vulnerability. I joke because I don't want to sound like a baby, but inside? Whole other ball game. Thank you for knowing. And if you didn't know, thank you for not judging.*

2010 | The faces look animated and bright on my walk down Seventh Avenue tonight.

Manhattan can affect your perception, especially when you're feeling angry, hurt, disappointed, depressed. At those times, the cheerful faces at the outdoor cafés can oppose aloneness. Their laughter can blot you out, rub it in: you are not of our happy ranks. This is the circus of pleasure and play. Where did you go wrong? But every face looks beautiful to me tonight. Maybe because I am tired of being sad, maybe because I've been reading a little Walt Whitman, who suddenly makes sense in a whole new way. This listing, this habit of naming what he sees, high and low, monumental and minuscule, raw and cooked—isn't he in fact inscribing boundaries in language? Isn't he saying *you're not me, and you're not me,* and finding delight in that? The exquisite loneliness of the poet striding down the sidewalk. How else could intimacy happen if we didn't carve boundaries between us? It is the great paradox of love, and I am making love begin as I say, *bearded young skateboarder zigzagging in and out through cars.* I am making love begin as I say, *old woman pushing shopping cart outside Duane Reade.* These were never figments of the One Holy Self, but real people, moving in time, cherished by someone, hated by someone, morphing, active, irreplaceable.

A prayer:
You who I don't know how to talk to anymore. You whose body comes to me in a dream only to be gone as soon as I say your face, your mouth, your arms, your breasts, your feet. What happens when you die? The broken light switch in the kitchen, the doorknob glistening in the saucer by the window. How can you get in? This solitude, no match for your solitude, which must want to be sung again in the clear strong throats of the living. You who must want to be useful again, now that the two of us can see the myths we made of ourselves. What use is this skin now that you no longer have it? Would you have lived differently, read other books, loved other men, spent more time

in the woods, the mountains, the sea? What happens when you die? Teach me to listen so that I might know what you know now.

2010 | There is a person in my house. In the passenger seat, at my chair at the dining room table. In my refrigerator, on the toilet seat, feet on the bathtub, hands on the sink. On my sofa, where his eyes fix on the TV screen. On my walk past the bookstore, the gallery. Between the rows of spinach and radish that I picked just weeks back, when the sun warmed the back of my neck. The person is a good cook. The person makes the rich food of the poor, delicious and caloric, high in oil, fat, and salt. The person takes the walk I just walked to the bay beach, where he meets the people I would have met, provoking wonder (and confusion, I'm sure) when he's leaning back into the arms of my Beloved.

Meanwhile, I am back in church, where I am singing the hymns with clear, powerful notes, in spite of the sore throat I've been nursing for a week. I sing without the least bit of fear. I sing without any tightness in the lower half of my face. I sing not louder than any of the others but with them, inside them.

And here I thought singing was hard. And here I thought singing was work, asking us to use parts of the body (lungs, throat, tongue, lips) that would so much rather be at rest than pouring out sound. I leave the church, having sung twenty songs and acclamations, and for a little while on my walk down West Sixteenth Street, I can swallow without any discomfort around the roof of my mouth, around the back of my uvula. All of that will change in a little while, but it's still a way off. I'll find out, days later, when I go to the doctor, that I have strep throat. I've been singing entire songs through strep throat, and it doesn't even hurt.

A day later S insists on showing the Beloved multiple DVDs of his acting and singing roles. Not just one performance, but a second and a third and a fourth and so on. Every male lead from every musical penned, from Lerner and Loewe through Sondheim. This goes on for an evening. So many performances that the poor Beloved is smothered in need—there is nothing less attractive than need, raw need, a desperate artist—and the Beloved drifts far away from the sofa, out the window, through the woods up to the clouds, and the cold dome of space, as lonely as he'd ever been.

As if this should foretell the end of the story? Well, perhaps. But the story is never linear, and this might only be another beginning.

September 28, 2008

My Darling,

Forgive me and ask M to forgive me, too, because I haven't written him to thank him yet for that wonderful letter, but it's been insane here. The pressure to get this tenure packet done under these physical constraints has truly been a challenge. Your cold sounded awful and I've got one, too. Not to mention the return of C-diff so now I'm back on medication.

Paul, this beautiful apartment has become a literal prison; I haven't been outside for over two weeks because of the stairs.

(I move on October 10. I was under so much stress that I moved my chemo date from Oct. 1 to Oct. 13. I figured it best to begin it in a place where I feel safe, where I can move around, have a washer/dryer, and can walk freely from room to room and NOT use a commode!!)

Anyway, I forgot that this Tuesday I must go to the brain oncologist for what they call an Inspection. I think this is when they determine whether or not the radiation is successful. I do know I have short term memory loss and trouble with numbers and sequencing. . . .

I hate to sound whiny and boring, but life has gotten

just a shade unwieldy and I'm trying to remain calm.
I think after the 10th? Life will start all over again. . . .

So, I don't think I'll be seeing you this week much as
I want to. Are you mad? I get so tired that it feels I only
have eight hours in a day instead of 24. My stamina
is nil.

I will write a civilized email soon. Forgive this but I
didn't want to be out of touch. . . .

I love you deeply.

One day the woman inside the apartment on the first floor
hears crying, crying from the second-floor landing. She sits still for a
minute. She listens, then cracks her door, just to make sure she hasn't
imagined it. Maybe it's just a cat, sound from a neighbor's TV. She
walks up the stairs. There Denise is curled against the wall, unable
to get up the last flight. Most likely Denise cries harder once she's
been seen like this. Somehow the woman leads-carries-leads her up
the stairs. She sits Denise down, she asks her if she wants a drink:
coffee, water, a glass of lemonade. She's so moved by the plight of
her neighbor that an idea comes to her on the spot—she'll trade her
apartment for Denise's sometime in the coming week. She's always
wanted to live at the top, while Denise has always wanted to be near
the leaves and water in the garden. The woman, after all, is a life
coach, and she couldn't call herself a life coach if she weren't willing
to make this sacrifice on her neighbor's behalf. Denise beams at the
woman's offer; maybe she even weeps. How could human beings, so
frequently unreliable, be capable of such goodness, such selflessness?
The woman leaves after Denise is settled, and that is the last Denise
will ever hear from her.

2010 | I don't leave my therapist's office without remarking that the
process ahead isn't going to be chronological. J nods with relief as
if I've said the gold star thing. Though human beings condition one

another to want order, peace, and resolution, we also don't want too much of that, and just when it seems all is comprehensible, the world bewilders us again. But before it bewilders me again, I grieve my old life with M, as I grieve my old life with Denise. I see Denise's body, her arms, her legs, walking toward me. To take care of me? The life that thought it was a given, the life that thought safety and routine were never up for question. Perhaps they should have always been up for question. Two writers together: what on earth were we thinking? Suddenly I see Denise's lost body all over again, as I talk to my therapist about making the link between her death and M's crisis. He was the first to see a possible link between the two crises; the image of Denise's approach in the daydream reinscribes that. "Smart man," I tell J.

Two hours after my session, M runs into a friend from way back, someone he'd once hooked up with, and it seems crucial that they meet now, immediately. We haven't seen each other for two days. I know they're not meeting for sex, but *still*. They are going out for a hamburger together. As to the dinner I'd been imagining with him? I leave the apartment. I walk west to the High Line. I trudge up the staircase, turn south past the fringetree, the smoketree, the quince. I look out to the Hudson, the late sun over Hoboken, Jersey City, the Statue of Liberty. The asters smolder as if they're about to burst into flame. I sit on the edge of a lounge chair. Okay, I should have asked earlier in the day if he'd wanted to go out for dinner. I just assumed he'd want to do what I wanted to do. But that doesn't stop the rage from heating up my face. I walk back down the High Line steps. Soon I am walking through the Meatpacking District, crossing the West Side Highway. Past the trees, the river, the benches where lovers sit, leaning into each other. The night is beautiful, hot. Waves pulse against the bulkhead, the air fresh with the smell of the ocean. Water plunges and lifts beneath the open metal grate. Still, it is New York City in July. What the hell am I doing in New York City in July, when I've spent every summer of my life near the ocean? The desire for the ocean has always come before anything, and I am hours from where I really want to be.

An hour later I am back inside the apartment. It's humid and stuffy inside, the air conditioner is off. M is on the sofa. *Hi*, he says. And I know my face is the color of heart attack, my peasant ancestors rising up in me. I ask for his hand and tell him how angry I am, how hard it is to say how angry I am. The two of us must look like monsters to each other, our faces clenched into unexpected shapes. This is not the way we've ever known each other, but it is the way we must behave if we're to accommodate conflict, not simply be the couple that looks happy from outside. The anger is as thick as musk in the air. My thoughts are out of sequence, or is this what it feels like to run sixty miles per hour into the side of a mountain? We are quiet for some minutes. The argument is not resolved. Tonight I don't think it will ever be resolved. I am in a complex position: To say I am jealous is to be possessive, to lack trust. To stay silent is to grow hurt in myself.

And when I stay silent, I am tested by M.

If there were any more freedom in this house, there wouldn't be a house.

I sit down with my laptop. I open the inbox, and ten sample covers of my novel come in from Kapo, my book designer. I click the icon. "Look," I say, and M glances over my shoulder, puts his glasses on. I start scrolling. As if no argument had ever transpired in that room, we sit side by side on the sofa, knee pressed into knee, and begin to talk about the sequence of twelve burning houses. For a while, we are back to our old sweet ways.

It Is Hard Work to Be Dead

2008 | Can it really be two months since I've last seen Denise? Her moving, my cold, her cold, *C. diff,* radiation, chemo, her move to a one-floor apartment—so many things standing in the way of us, even though we've talked a lot on the phone and sent messages to each other. I don't want any of my fear to show on my face. I know she will look different; she has been through so much since my last visit—will she even be the Denise I know? I try to relax the muscles in my face as I walk up the steps to the new building. I speak my name, as calmly as I can, to the doorman behind the desk.

And there she is at her door. She is looking hard at my face to see how she might look, and I am watching myself, trying to let her know that, no, I'm not shocked that she's thinner. I'm not shocked that she's blond. Denise, of all people, blond. Not that she chose blond, but blond's the color of the soft hair that's come in after chemo. Her hair is like the down on a chick, so impossibly new that you might not even want to bring her out into the world. If she could have foreseen this transformation from an earlier point in her life, maybe she'd have enjoyed that trip to Wisconsin more. There she swore that everyone looked at her as if she were trouble. So dark, so *Sicilian*—they stood back a few feet from her, as if certain she'd put a curse on their families, or worse.

I stop thinking about her hair. If there's anything that shocks me, it's the apartment itself, which is certainly a good apartment, facing west toward the Schuylkill, with large windows opening to the western sky and the playing fields of the University of Pennsylvania. But it doesn't look like an apartment that she'd put together. All of her things are here, her chests, her paintings, but it doesn't have—

what? Her love, her sense of making a work of art out of her home. The rooms feel temporary, with none of the full range of her personality, as if a group of well-meaning people had approximated her personality for her and she was too tired and compromised to care. The apartment's a way station, and that is a notion I find hard to bear. But she distracts me from any of that, and within minutes, we're sitting on her sofa, looking out to the sky, watching a September thunderstorm flashing, pretending that we're much more scared than we actually are.

2010 | It's not the biggest shock to find out that M is getting a dog. After all, we've talked of getting a dog for six years, ever since we lost Arden. Arden had many functions in our lives. Uncle, child, brother, friend—all these things and more, and maybe we were honoring his absence by traveling, by doing all the things we couldn't do when he was sick. It was freeing to move again, without thinking of him being left behind, resting his head on his paws on some concrete kennel floor. But if you're a person who has loved a dog, you can't live so long without sharing your bed with another creature. You miss the routines (feeding, walking); you miss meeting the people you wouldn't talk to without a dog. You don't know how much you're giving up simply by keeping yourselves alone.

But a golden retriever? I keep quiet as he tells me about the breeder on the phone. Hadn't I once said that I wanted a blond French bulldog? A German shepherd, a pit bull, an English bull, a boxer, a beagle: any breed but a golden retriever, all goof and wiggle. A golden retriever, the kind of dog who rolls in the slop, runs toward you, wiping the slop on your best jeans, expecting you to find him endearing. I want a dog with spine. I want a dog with gravitas, a dog with a little shadow in his face and walk, eager for boundaries and conditions and agreements, if not for you, then for himself. Any creature, canine or human, deserves the joys of accomplishment.

And yet there's no turning back for M. In spite of my anger

about S (I still refuse to go out to the Springs house, which I think of as my lost house, the closet still full of my shirts, my study still packed with school books, teaching papers, bank statements), I don't discourage him, especially as he's as nervous as he is excited about the appointment to come. Life with a dog. A walk in the morning, a walk in the afternoon, filling food bowls, thinking about a dog, missing a dog, the kind of looking and listening any human could use, especially those of us who think of ourselves as too busy, with no time for anything more.

What must it be like to take that ride he's on? Trees going by, brake lights ahead, burning. The stomach burning, or maybe empty, as who could eat on the verge of changing your life, another life? Then to park, to walk into the breeder's. To see the puppy in the play-pen, back warmed by the white fur on his brother's stomach, and the face tilted up to see you for the first time—that first *who are you?* cock of the head that literally grounds you to yourself.

I am dog. Who are you?

Smell of sawdust in the air. Biscuit, flour, corn muffin, a little ammonia in the mix. Pee? The smell of puppy.

Why am I not standing in that room with him?

I press my head hard, harder into my hand. The solutions to our problems seem even further away now. They're out on some island and the boat has left without us.

2008 | I can't tell whether Denise's health situation is better, or whether it's in some holding pattern. Maybe we're just pretending it's in a holding pattern. It's definitely easier to live that way than the other, which says that death is inevitable, so it's time to start getting one's books in order. Denise is having no such thing, and maybe that's why she seems to be the model cancer patient. Maybe that's why she's taking higher doses of chemo and radiation than was thought possible for someone of her age and weight. I can believe she's going to go on and on, as I am not seeing her every day. The story of I'll-be-around-longer-than-you-think requires physical separation, and imaginative faith from both parties. And maybe that's why a month or two after her death, Denise's ex sends me a folder of photographs from her final months, without any words attached. Just a folder in my inbox. The Denise in these photographs is not pretty or composed, even though she could be those things during those months, her hair short and blond: half Annie Lennox, half professor of women's literature. You can see pain in her face, tension hardening her mouth. You can see her trying to feel better when family fills the kitchen, though she feels anything but. I can't help but feel a stab of helplessness. Denise wouldn't want me to see her this way. But maybe there's value in getting to see what it was like for those who were there for her, by her side, night in and night out. Denise looks around as if to say, who are these helpers in my house? And why are their coats and bags on my bureau, my table? My apartment, the apartment I once called my own.

2010 | I check my computer to see that my mail program has updated itself. Somehow syncing it to my phone has disrupted everything, and six years of emails disappear between five o'clock and six, without any warning. Not only the addresses but the messages themselves, messages I've been unknowingly using as a kind of journal, whenever I needed to see what I was thinking on, say, Christmas Eve 2004. Inside the lost mailbox is much of my correspondence with Denise. As troubling as losing it sounds, I'm in the frame of mind where I'm not shattered—though I am curious about not feeling shattered. How many times have I read her letters, heard her voice on the page, so certain of its persistence, its ability to keep on? Maybe Denise's messages, maybe the messages of any of the people now dead, are best consigned to the ether. Probably I am thinking there will be a way to get all those emails back, an adjustment of a server setting, a reconfiguration of a password. But I must think about what I'd do if I couldn't get them back. Would I be okay enough to go on without her written voice, no chance to read them some July, ten years from now, on her birthday? Sure, I might think I'm okay with it tonight, when I'm sitting in the chair by the open window with a glass of red wine in hand. None of the old fears of loss stirring up panic. But maybe it won't be okay ten years from now when someone asks me who she was to me, and I've just turned her into some myth, so many versions away from the person I knew.

It helps to be asked who she is to me, even now when it hasn't even been a year yet. In an email one night, Braunwyn asks, *I need to know, I don't understand.* She is wondering about Denise's importance to me. Have I talked about her that much? And the starkness of her confusion brings me back to familiar ground: What must it be like for Braunwyn to walk in the shoes of the dead? Or better said, to walk on after the dead? It's a territory I know. Walking on as another version of my mother's twin, Paul, killed in a car accident at seventeen. Walking on as another version of M's lover, dead at forty-two. Of course, we're all walking in the steps of the dead, but it's different to play that role for someone who's lost another person. Replacements are never as good as the dead—we never can be. We've never achieved that level of perfection—that story with an ending. Closure, as it's called. We have faults, we feel them burning inside us, wanting to fly out, to twist our mouths. So we end up keeping those fires inside. We don't let our lover or mother see those fires. They already have too much on their minds, too much worry in their hearts. They don't need to know that we're jealous, maybe sometimes even resentful of the power and purity of the dead in their hearts. We know these are ugly feelings, we know we would like to be remembered, so we just make ourselves small, smaller, until we shrink to the tiniest light.

Yes, this is how I will care for you. I will tune out my light and tune out my light until the fire stays completely inside, maybe unreachable to you. It doesn't even occur to me that you might want to warm your hands on that fire, that you might need it in order to forget.

And so I tell Braunwyn all about Denise. She, of course, has heard all the stories; she knows all about how I wouldn't be writing without her; she knows about that last year in which we became closer. But it is different to say it clearly, directly. And in the clearly and directly I'm also able to say what was difficult about Denise, about our friendship. I tell Braunwyn about her competitive streak. I tell her she wasn't always a good listener. I tell her about Denise's volatility, her insecurity, her need to be affirmed—how many times a day? But in saying it like that, it doesn't feel as if I am betraying her. It is the first time I've said such things without feeling bad about myself. The acknowledgment of her complexity feels like love, and if that means Denise is just a little further away from me right now, then . . .

I like to think of what M said on the day of my mother's funeral mass. He said he saw my mother sitting on the bed of the old motel in Pompano Beach, exhausted from having visited so many people. *It is hard work to be dead,* he said she said—or approximately that. She needed a rest. She wanted a cup of tea. But the most arresting thing? She could lean in and listen without judgment. For the first time she could look at people—even the people closest to her—without judgment. And that, according to M, is the great, great blessing of the dead.

In asking these questions, Braunwyn is doing her part to pull me down to earth. She says, look at my face, I am here. This is all we have.

2010 | I can't foresee that my new friendship with Braunwyn will fall apart weeks after the summer is out. She'll want more than I'm able to give, though she'll insist that that's not true. She'll want so much that I'll sag under the weight of disappointing her. Over and over, she makes me feel as if I am disappointing her.

I take the train to meet her at her house in Montclair. I play with her two dogs; I hang out with her husband, her son. We have the nicest times when we go out to restaurants, but we cannot seem to have an in-depth conversation without Braunwyn pulling the subject back to M. Over and over the subject comes back to M, which is magnetizing in the early days—I don't want to hate this new M—but confusing finally. The worst version of him is reflected back to me and I cannot say I like it. I will always be protective of M, especially against any version that wants to simplify him. She keeps saying she can identify with him, at the same time she makes him seem a little like a monster. He is not a monster. And yet I can't shake her admission, spoken with soft, bemused pride, that every relationship she's counseled through a difficult patch has ended up in divorce. By the time I'm getting back on the train, I'm down again. My mouth tastes of dirt. I can't even lift my head to look at the houses and lights going by. And what of the apartment she wants to rent together in Ocean Grove this winter? I think of her face on the night of my birthday, intent, expectant, as if in wait for me to say: let's run away. By September I'll stop returning her emails and calls, but not without missing her and feeling just awful about it.

So I turn to my old friend Marie. I walk over to her place on Barrow Street some nights and we talk. The apartment is a little like a boat, a white boat, floating on the tops of the trees. From the living room sofa you can see the Empire State Building. The lights at the top are blue tonight. Sometimes I read to her daughter, Inan, who lies on her stomach, on the pink rag rug, head down, listening. Sometimes Marie and I hang out in her tiny kitchen, drinking seltzer, eating watermelon. A breeze blows through the open window. I am at home here, even if I only stop by a couple of hours a week. Marie must know that that's necessary.

And there's Elizabeth. Though she's in Austin, she might as well be around the block from me. I talk to her all the time on the phone. We exchange long, involved emails. She has known M and me since the beginning; she knows more than anyone how broken up I am. She expresses concern when she finds out that I've lost twenty-five pounds in less than two months. She is not afraid to make me laugh, though. No one can make me laugh like Elizabeth. Her irreverence is as necessary as rain, and I try to say funny things back to her in my head, even when I'm just looking at the faces passing by on the sidewalk.

2010 | I step off the train and spot him instantly: I believe he is the smallest golden retriever I've ever seen. His hair is like the hair on a chick, but thicker. He is down at the foot of the ramp, beside M, who gives me a hug, a big hug. I put down my bag and crouch. I say, hey, *hey*, to the dog in front of me. He looks everywhere but at my face; he jumps at the slam of a van door, wrenches his head to listen to a song sparrow. I reach out to hold him around his ribs. For a second he makes eye contact with me, then sneezes all over my face. I laugh, I approve of its spray. A lady from the other side of the parking lot laughs; she approves of it, too. I am overstimulated. It's my first visit back to Springs since S left for good—the first time in over a month—and so many feelings are playing out; they are canceling one another out. I am wary of coming back home. We are drawing closer again; is our separation coming to a close? Whatever the case, it is good to have a new dog around to distract and center us, to help us though yet another transition.

We stop at a coffee place. During our time on the front porch, the dog won't look at me for more than a second at a time. We head home. The dog won't look at me for the rest of the afternoon, into the night. All that changes the next morning when rustlings wake me up at five thirty, and I step out of the bed to see the creature looking up at me. He's slapping his tail so hard against the flagstone floor that it must hurt. And what is your name? I say, as I kneel before him, the dense weight of his head pressing against my breastbone. So many names held up and cast aside: Clark, Grant, Buddy, Lars, Nils, Sven, Stig, Luke, but somehow only Ned seems to work. He's been called Ned so many times now that it would seem false to add another name to the list, even though the name seems to mean as much to him as *cake* or *twig* or *switchblade.* How long will it take before he answers to his name?

In days I am caught up in life with Ned. Ned on the front porch of the Springs General Store, Ned at the coffee bar in Montauk, Ned squeaking through a hole in the deer fence, Ned falling in the fish pond, Ned falling headfirst into the toilet as he's trying to take a drink. Ned growling at Clarabelle, an elderly dog with cancer—unfamiliar walk? candied, chemical smell? Sickness, death—this must be the first time he's coming into contact with mortality, at least among his kind. Maybe he isn't even barking at the dog herself, but at what's inside her, the death that wants to take her down, take him down. This knowledge is just where life begins, though no one, not even a three-month-old puppy, wants to be confronted with that.

Ned beside me as I'm standing at the toilet, and his face looking up to meet mine, and instantly he pees, too, but right on the floor tile, beside my left sneaker.

The three of us are in our respective places in the car, heading west through Queens into the city for errands and appointments and what will turn out to be Ned's first Manhattan trip. The anxiety of it, the excitement—or perhaps it's just the dire intensity of the past five weeks—has sharpened me. My consciousness is a fresh pencil point, and every sense, every impression gets written down and named. The Unisphere in Flushing Meadows Park seems weird to me all over again, as I hold Ned on my lap. He looks out in the general direction of the fair. Joni's *Night Ride Home* is playing on the stereo. Occasionally, I sing along, and am surprised by how many of the lines I know, as I'd never thought it was one of her best albums. But just as M and I are singing "Come In from the Cold," I understand this album, this particular sequence of songs in a way I'd never gotten them before. Each song a coming to terms with the end of youth, the end of sex, or at least a certain kind of sex that leads us to places where we don't always want to go. (Denise and her golfer, Denise and

Famous Writer, Denise and the next-door neighbor.) But it's terrible to move beyond all that, because it feeds us just as it depletes us, right? *Is this just vulgar electricity or the edifying fire?* It's all there in those nine words, and I think both M and I feel the question in exactly the same way, at the same time. I'm sure anyone in the cars to the right or left of us would look in at us and think, look at those two singing so unself-consciously. Could there be a happier couple? And just as the Empire State Building rises over the road ahead of us, that thought catches in my throat, and I'm holding on to the dog in my lap, missing the life I once thought I'd lived. I thought I was happier—than anyone.

Damage

2008 | Only days away from the end of the fall term, and I'm already thinking toward the three months we're going to spend in Palo Alto, California, where M has a guest appointment at a university. I haven't been too keen on any guest appointment ever since North Carolina. Part of that simply has to do with having bad luck with living spaces, houses that don't feel conducive to concentration and focus and sitting still. Not that one should be surprised by that. No one who truly loves his house packs up his things and rents to strangers for five months every year. But it is impossible to say no to California, with its palms and plants and promise of sunlight. I must know on a certain level that I want to step out of my life, my mother's illness. In just a few weeks, she'll break her hip after a fall in the night, and we won't know whether she'll be able to stay on at Ranmar Gardens, the assisted living facility; she might need more care than that. And Denise? Well, of course I want to be nearby. I want to be closer than the hour-and-twenty-minute train ride from New York. But I also want to be on the other side of the continent, far away from illness and decay, where trees are beginning to bud, and where redwoods grow beside palms and blooming bougainvillea, even at the coldest point of the year, when the sun is lowest in the sky.

"And how long are you going to be in California?" Denise says.

There's a longer-than-usual silence after I tell her two months, which isn't exactly the truth. Instinctively, I know not to say ten weeks.

"Okay," she says, considering. There's a pragmatic quality to her yes, an achieved sense of neutrality that isn't the Denise of old. The Denise of old would have let her disappointment be known, maybe not directly, but indirectly, and it might not have always been pretty.

But the delay in her response isn't about disappointment. Negotiation is deeper than disappointment, which is why she might take the conversation back to small things, to Christmas presents and where we might buy black ribbon and silver wrapping paper.

2010 | Another headline: SIGNS OF REGROWTH SEEN IN LOUISIANA MARSH.

Headlines like these are everywhere right now, almost four months after the Gulf oil spill began, and they're not just coming from right-wing, pro-business operations, but from organizations that claim to care about the environment, the health of children, the elderly, the animals. I wonder how many people read past the headlines; the narrative certainly doesn't promise an involving story. Maybe we simply don't have it in us to say that things don't get better. Maybe, in America at least, we have a hard time living with the notion that anything might stay the same, or get worse, for that matter, no matter how many cynical statements we might use to protect ourselves. No matter how many small businesses go bankrupt, no matter how many libraries close in the inner cities, no matter how many bombs are dropped, or people jailed and tortured overseas.

But it might not be that simple. Maybe such reports have a deeper purpose. Maybe they want to tell us it is okay to do damage because damage is never permanent. It doesn't alter cell structures, it doesn't break minds or souls or bones, because it wants to tell us that growth is always stronger than death. Pour ammonia on the trunk of a tree, and look, sprouts at the top of that blackened trunk! Cause and effect? Who says that one thing necessarily begets another? The forces that move the world along might be much more complicated, more random and omnidirectional, than we've begun to know.

There's the president, swimming with his daughters in the Gulf, just to show the country that we've put all this trouble behind us. Click goes the camera, and the faces of his children travel all over the world in a second.

Maybe the harder thing is to recognize that growth might not happen without a little damage first. I say that from the position of someone who would do anything not to do damage, even though some of that might be entirely out of my hands.

A few months back I spent a week in Florida, mostly on the west coast, which I hadn't seen since my twenties. I'd written off that part of Florida as unfriendly, socially conservative. I saw no reason ever to go back, and yet there I was, on a tour of colleges in the Tampa Bay area. I was at dinner with my friends Ira and Katie and two of their grad students, and we got to talking about Florida, more specifically the Florida of armadillos and wood storks, pygmy rattlers and any of the creatures or plants that remind residents they're not just anywhere. It occurred to me that this was the Florida that had riveted my childhood imagination. It was the Florida I'd forgotten after having spent so much time in sculpted, manmade Broward County, where my parents had settled, so denatured that I hadn't even been bitten by a mosquito in fifteen years. So on a Saturday morning, I spent an hour in a wildlife sanctuary on the south shore of Charlotte Harbor, in Punta Gorda. I got out of the car. I walked toward the boardwalk. As soon as I stepped onto the planks through the mangroves, I caught myself welling up. I knew I could have stayed in those trees for hours, all day in fact, the sun warming my arms, the wind pushing the leaves around. What was it I'd left behind? The question seemed insurmountable, and I wanted it back, whatever it was. Far out into the harbor, past sailboats and channel markers, three dolphins stitched the surface then went under, and stayed under. I didn't see them again, though I kept looking. And deep in cold water, where I couldn't possibly see her, a manatee scoured the channel for plants.

2009 | I tell myself I like Palo Alto. I like its Arts and Crafts houses. I like its walking downtown, its intricate, inhabited gardens, its neighborhoods of Eichler houses (Greenmeadow, Fairmeadow), but I can't stop getting lost. It takes genuine mental effort to say that west is toward the mountains, maybe because the town wasn't built on a north-south-east-west grid, but wrenched to the left and up, so I never quite know where I am on the map. The second time I go for a run I get bold enough to take a shortcut past the elementary school, and the next thing I know, I've made several wrong turns. I don't know where east is. I don't know where downtown is, and the live oaks are so dense in this part of town that I can't even see the mountains. It feels as if I've wandered into a genteel piece of Beverly Hills that broke off and floated several hundred miles to the north, and there isn't a person in sight. All life seems to transpire behind palms and walls and windows with their shades pulled down, and it certainly doesn't help that I don't have any identifiers in my pocket or on my person, no wallet, no cell phone, no GPS. Of course I end up finding my own way, but it takes a good hour. I'm so humbled I literally jump at the sight of two seven-year-old girls who leap out from behind a parked Volkswagen as a joke. My feet are chafed and sore inside my sneakers, and along with my sense of direction, I wonder whether I've lost my sense of humor.

After two weeks I fly back east to see Denise. I step over filthy crusts of snow as I walk down the streets. I walk past blocks of brick row houses on—Walnut Street? Locust? I have a clear sense of how long those houses have been around, how many different generations and cultures have passed by their long, many-paned windows. (Wealthy neighborhood, less-wealthy neighborhood, poor neighborhood, up-and-coming neighborhood . . .) They also strike me as bleak, in spite of their classical symmetry, but maybe that's the stripped trees, the empty, soundless sidewalks. It's probably a good sign that nothing else about our four hours together stays with me. I must be inside the visit, sitting inside our talking, looking out at a sky that promises snow but won't deliver snow. I'm not already interpreting, representing our day. I have every reason to think we'll have years ahead of days like this—sweet, unremarkable days. And it's only when I dig up a letter that I see a different story about that day.

My friend.

January 28, 2009

We are on a wavelength today. I just sat at the computer to tell you I had the best time today and love you so much I can't even begin to find words. You have been the best friend to me always and my brother and my dream love. Your eyes just sparkle with intelligence and mischief and kindness and loyalty. I am going to have March 20 as my goal to come to NYC to hear you read.

Paul, do you know I had only looked at the top half of the front page of the Times *and didn't even see that Updike died! I saw the publishing piece and went right to that never even glancing down at the bottom of the first page.* Rabbit Run *is still one of my favorite novels and the short story "Separating" in* Too Far to Go *still breaks my heart. The ending of it was so daring and so painful. All those Joan and Richard Maple stories gathered in one collection feel like a novel.*

I remember being beside myself with joy when Updike and Cheever appeared together on the Dick Cavett Show. *Oh, I was in heaven.*

Anyway, today was superlative!

I keep thinking there was something else you wanted to tell me about your teaching and I interrupted. Just smack me if I do that again.

Okay. More later. I'm sending all good energy.

Biggest love to you,
xoxoxoxoxoxoxo

2009 | A sweet evening in San Francisco. M and I are walking down a street, an unusually quiet street in Chinatown, when a young woman pulls up behind a double-parked car and holds down the horn. She holds it for a good twenty seconds. It is the nastiest horn I've ever

heard. An elderly man with a walker is being maneuvered into the
backseat of that double-parked car, and the sight of the young woman's twisted face is enough to stir up an animal panic in us. "You
stop that," M says with a decisive gesture, and the Chinese people
just look at us with bemusement, as if they might be used to these
dark altercations, where Chinatown collides with North Beach. But
the raging young woman doesn't like to be told what to do by two
men, especially two men whom she decides to call faggots. Words
are volleyed back and forth, she pulls ahead, and to our shock, she's
parked the car. She's walking back, walking right back up to M to call
him a faggot. Over and over so it sounds like the verbal equivalent
of a knife striking skin. We curse back, which only makes matters
worse. Human confrontation without boundaries, without control.
I cry out, "What happened to your soul?," which I know is ludicrous
and darkly funny as I say it, straight out of Flannery O'Connor. Still,
I really want to know what would make a human being that mad.
She walks down the street, across Columbus Avenue to a restaurant
with outside tables. We keep walking. And the next thing we know
six guys are heading toward us, with shoulders squared, in a row,
as if in the opening sequence of some TV crime drama. The raging
woman has summoned these six guys, so we duck into the first door
we see: a small empty restaurant. We're laughing and frightened and
stunned all at once—this is too absurd. We tell the waiters we're
being followed. They say, *We'll hide you. Of course, of course we'll
hide you*, until they see their *boss* coming in through the front door.
Their boss is one of the six men. The boss owns the restaurant we've
chosen to hide in, oh God. Certainly we can project into the future
and can see the comic insanity of the situation transpiring in front
of us—isn't this situation right out of a movie, or a parody of some
movie? At the same time, we're aware of how close we are to getting
killed—or, if not killed, seriously beaten up. We're told to step outside, which sounds like an invitation to fight, and we say no, we're not
going to fight. We're going to stand right here until the anger in the

atmosphere dissipates. This sequence happens over and over, until we're finally out of the restaurant, out on the sidewalk, into the chilly night. We're told that the Castro is on the other side of Market. We're called some names, some ridiculous names and some that hurt. And this is San Francisco? A smell of dog fear follows us as we walk down Columbus. We hail a cab. We go back to the guesthouse. We walk up the stairs, open the door, bolt the door, sit on the bed. I am out of breath. Any humor or distance about the situation fades to quiet and numbness. I turn on the eleven o'clock news, but I can't keep my attention on the mouths moving on the screen. And at some point—is it that night? or is it sometime the next morning?—the two of us try to describe what happened on our blogs.

Not the most brilliant move. It takes all of a few hours for another blog to pick up the story. The story is simplified, and soon enough the situation isn't ours anymore, but a broad outline, a broad version of a story told over and over again—just the particulars are different this time. San Francisco. Such things are not supposed to happen in San Francisco, capital of benevolence and open-mindedness. The city newspaper passes on the story, and then another. Comment after comment appears on the restaurant's Yelp page. There are calls for gay people, straight people, to boycott said restaurant. A volcano is spewing. True, it is a small volcano in the realm of volcanoes, but it is a volcano nonetheless, bits of ash and fire falling on so many foreheads now. Things only shift a bit when the restaurant owner—or his associate—and I come to some peace in the comment field on M's blog. I remind him that the argument started as part of a defense of sick people—it was never about name-calling, it was never about restaurant boycotts. I say, my mother has broken her hip. Wouldn't you want someone to stand up for you if someone you knew were in that position? It sounds self-righteous, I know. But I want this to come to some use, some peace. Besides, I can think of no other way to stop the flow of it, which keeps slopping all over the web: an uncapped well. Neither one of us has listened to the other. Beneath our rage and pride, two strangers reach out to each other, or attempt to.

For some reason I don't tell any of this to Denise. Am I just embarrassed to have taken part in a confrontation that somehow became public? Maybe, simply, there is no need to tell her about grace exchanged between two people. Grace—she knows enough about that.

April 6, 2009

Hi Honey,

I've been wanting to write a long, coherent, love-filled, chatty email to you for days. You'll be happy to know I've ordered ALL Louise DeSalvo books. And thank you so much for the compliment about her being so Denise Gess. Happy to hear M's New Brunswick event went well. I know. I do so love the Rutgers students, too. I'm just happy for both of you.

I thought of you through my sore throat/mouth because I know how much you hate/fear them. I must say the Magic Mouthwash does work. It numbs the pain so well that I'm afraid I'm going to bite my tongue as it sloshes around. But all is improving, including my mood and my determination to get on with the business of writing. I've wasted too much time away from my work. Enough! I say.

I am pleased to announce that I am now a tenured, Associate Professor. Yay! The way the cancer's been proceeding I have some doubt about my ability to teach in the fall, but it's too soon to tell. The promo will give me enough disability salary (2/3 of pay) to keep me at this income level and make it possible to live/pay bills/have insurance.

Paul, I love love love your table! It reminds me of my old table too but I believe yours is a better table in terms of square nails, patina, etc. Oh, I can't wait to get out there if you'll still have me in the spring. The gift I have for you and M is truly perfect especially now that I see the table in the room. If I have to hire a driver to get to you I will! How much are drivers anyway? I will be going to Chatham for 4th of July so that's something to look forward to. A friend has a small private plane which makes traveling to Chatham easy, fast and fun!

I'm so glad you got your contract. I can't thank you enough for thinking of me for that anthology. You are a tremendous support. You've no idea how much it means to me.

Send me your addresses again, too. I don't have an excuse for misplacing mine—except chemo brain. Send the NYC and Springs. I can't wait for new CDs!!!!! You're my musical mentor, you know. My G-U-R-U.

I assume you saw Bernard Cooper's essay in the Times *magazine section—was it last week? Loved it. And did you read that piece on the necessity of the short story in the Business section yesterday? An unlikely place for the piece but I loved it. I wish I'd reviewed the Cheever bio; I reviewed the Donaldson book years ago on him and loved it. I think this one delves deeper?*

Okay, honey. More later. I think of you always too and am so glad you're in my life!

Love to M.

> *Love, love*
> *your D always xxxxxoooo*

Bye

2009 | A clear scrubbed sky without any moisture in it. Leaves darker, greener, and more resilient than just a few days before. Tree pollen inside our nostrils, on our lashes and lips, and maybe that makes my father's phone call easier to bear. He is crying, crying about my mother and her health, the turn it's taken, and for the first time he's asking me to fly to Florida, as in tomorrow—he's never said such things during any of her recent health crises. Should I come? I'd been so used to saying that question, so used to hearing him say no; maybe I thought his confidence would somehow see her through, would lift her and work on her. I'm not used to hearing this vulnerability in his voice. The last time he sounded like this was after my mother's mastectomy seven years before. Instinctively, I go into neutral. I must be strong and sane for us, for her. Not one tear falls down my face. I soak in the yard outside the restaurant where I'm standing: the green, green grass; the gravel parking lot; the white picnic benches; the people biting meticulously into their dosas. From here on out, that will be the texture of emergency to me, that calmness and beauty, and well-dressed mothers passing plates of healthy food to their children.

The plane flies low over the artificial canals of Sunrise and Plantation as it approaches the airport. I snap a shot of the wing of the plane, and I'm not surprised that the shot looks as blurry as my interior state. Everything is blurry: the back of the seat in front of me, the magazine on my tray table, the flight attendant walking down the aisle with a dazed, serene smile beneath her curtain of blond.

The next morning, my brothers, father, and I are in my mother's room, where she's lying unconscious. Bobby, who's already beside her in a chair, hides his face with the fingers of his right hand when he sees us walking into the room. His shoulders shake. I have not seen Bobby cry since childhood, decades back. He always has a good joke, even for the darkest things, for somebody's bad luck, someone's stupid line, an irritating neighbor's death. The jokes aren't exactly mean. They never intend to be black, and of course there's the slightest thrill about aiming straight into the heart of taboo. The jokes are also a way of making the moment in front of us bearable. Bobby? Where are your jokes right now? Why aren't you making us laugh?

There's not much to say in the face of a mother's death. We shift and we jitter. We're not at ease. How could we be? The four of us crowd the tight little bedroom of the assisted living facility, which smells of chicken broth, hand cream, old blankets. Air that hasn't been stirred by a breeze for so long. Her things are on the walls, on the bureau. A painting she did of a dog and a rubber ball. A small photograph of herself in a red coat. (No pictures of us? She needs to remember who *she* was first.) A hospice nurse walks in. She has the practiced demeanor of a good hospice nurse, detached and kind, and she handles the questions my brother Michael asks her, questions that are impossible to answer, but answers that anyone would want to know. How is she feeling? Is she in pain? How long will this process take? And just as she's ready to walk out the door, she turns to say that the dying need to be reassured that we're going to be okay without them. She sees it all the time, dying people hanging on, long past the time their bodies are ready to go. The advice is so sound, so true to my mother's character that I'm sure the light shifts in the room. Nothing seems to have changed out the window; the century plant and the datura are still there, but I see better. And smell the Lipton being steeped in the kitchen.

How do we let her know that we will go on without her? It's easier to do than we'd think, easier to enact than to say it straight on. The four of us sit around her bed, haphazardly remembering. The early years. The time the boat ran out of gas, and Vic Forte, our neighbor next door, showing up in his boat to tow us back home. Old restaurants along the Black Horse Pike on the way to the shore house: Pat's Tavern, Ann's Tavern, Finnerty's Hut, Tony's. Storybookland. The Race Track. Forest fires: the smell of them, the stinging in our eyes, the taste of smoke, and our animal reaction. Our first memories: mine? Choking on a penny I'd picked up from the pink bathroom floor and swallowed. The sides of the coin muscling down my throat. The taste: part spit, part blood, a little dirt, some yellow Dial soap, like nothing I'd ever tasted. And my father's palm slapping my back until my ribs and lungs hurt, as if that were the one true way to dislodge anything.

Her eyes stay open as if she wants us to keep going.

Maybe it's easier to make contact with her now that her language is out of the way. In recent years, any exchange with her has been puzzled by what dementia had done to her ability to interpret and speak, and though we tried not to judge what came out of her mouth, I'm sure she took our reactions in. Of course she took them in. My mother and her "inferiority complex," a phrase she'd used often about others, though she was too proud to apply it to herself. The barrier must have frustrated her. Now she looks at each of us in the room—first my father, then Bobby, Michael, then me—with her strong, steady gaze, and just for a minute we have the old mother back. She is taking each one of us in, in a way she hasn't done in years. She might not know who we are. We could be the police. We could be the president of the United States. We could be her parents, twin brother, her childhood friend, Bridgie Carey. But she does know we're beside her now. She does know we're Loved Ones.

But there is that instant when language returns. I get up to leave before my father and Michael leave. "Bye," I say to the room in general. "Bye!" my mother says in an unlikely voice, in an almost animal voice, as if it takes great effort to pull up that sound from her chest. And we laugh some to hear her come back for just a second from the place she's already on the way to.

Two nights later, an email from Denise:

May 19, 2009

Paul, she looks like a famous actress in this picture. I'm so glad I got to meet and spend time with her and that Austen met her, too. She made spaghetti for us. With meatballs!

If it's any comfort to you, please know that if your dad said she looked peaceful, she really was.

I remember feeling so relieved when I arrived at my mom's and saw my dad, truly peaceful, untortured, rested, nearly beatific. I reached out to kiss his face, held it in my hands, amazed at how finally after so many years of suffering and struggle, he'd been released from that body and I could actually see that he must have sighed, closed his eyes happily and had no pain. That image, holding him, helped me feel joy for him.

I just called you and left a message on the 917 number. I wanted to hear your voice and hear you say everything and anything you have to say. I think I might have the 713 # on my cell phone. I'll have to check.

There will be much to do tonight and tomorrow. My brother is coming for a brother/sister dinner, but you know I'm up late so feel free to call late if you like.

I don't want to bug you, but I want you to know I'm here for you.

Love,

D xxxxxooooo

2010 | One day, halfway through an email, a friend asks, what are the benefits of being an elegist? What does one get from taking on that role, playing the part of the rememberer? I lift my face from my laptop and stare at the dry ivy in the planter on the window ledge. A baby is crying down on the sidewalk. It's hot in the kitchen. I don't have words for her question, not right away at least. I might be annoyed. I'm wondering if she's suggesting that there are pitfalls, dangers I should watch out for. I certainly don't want to look admirable. I don't want to seem as if I'm someone to be held in high regard. I also don't want to seem as if I am of dignified character, because I am focusing on someone else, rather than myself. This is love as perfection. The dead person can't talk back, can't show up late for a dinner date, can't sit there with food on her face, with sour breath. None of the day-to-day uncertainty between people, nothing fraught with the possibilities of hurt feelings and one person misunderstanding the other. Gone, gone are the dead. Unreachable, transformed. Ash. Smoke. Bone chips. And no wonder the stories we tell about them stir up in our loins a positive charge, a reminder that we're not numb yet.

2009 | My mother loved to take the three of us on day trips. "Rides," she called them. Ten miles from home, twenty. She could never sit still. The destination was less important than the looking along the way. The little shacks and trees. The duck blinds and the abandoned developments and the sand roads into the pines. I wonder if she's relieved to move again now that she's dead. She'd spent so much time inside. Think of it: fourteen months in a chair, or in a bed. Not moving since she visited her condo that final time. There she sat on the violet living room sofa she'd once picked out the upholstery for, hands folded on her lap as if she were sitting in the house of a difficult stranger, who insisted she be well behaved, though that stranger never deigned to show herself. And once those two hours were up, and it was time to go back to assisted living, she seemed more than ready to go.

Two days after my mother's death, M and I hike the Seal Haulout Trail in Montauk State Park, following a path that's sometimes marked, sometimes not, sometimes dwindling off into bog and stream. Stones and roots make walking a challenge. Our arches already hurt in our shoes. Beech, vernal pool, muck, skunk cabbage, daylily, lichen, boulder. Splash. A frog? Maybe a frog, or a turtle going under. But later we definitely see a living creature, from a few hundred feet away: a seal out in the rocks in Block Island Sound. She holds us in her attention, with a whiskered, beagle-like face. I wave back. She keeps looking, then plunges her head beneath the surface. She comes up again, surprised we're still there, but more interested finally in the boat idling nearby. She must be thinking of the dangers of the boat, the possibility of it running over her, the importance of staying away. She appears to be the last of her kind around. The water is already too warm for the likes of her here. They're already up in Maine, the Bay of Fundy, Newfoundland. I watch her for as long as I can before we turn and head back up the mown path beside the woods.

The woods. Fly sounds, bird sounds, leaf flutter. The droning of bees in a shadbush grove. Violet butterfly, no wider than my thumbnail, flying leaf to leaf to leaf. And just around the corner, a hairy creature in the water: bronze, substantial, pointing its face away from us. A beaver? Dam in the making? I know beavers are out here—the local paper says there's a lone one in Scoy Pond a few miles away. Last summer one was run over by a car on the North Fork. But a sighting is too good to be true. I try for a picture, but the creature goes under and stays under, and I never get a look at her tail, the deciding factor. Maybe the creature is simply a muskrat; muskrats are much more common in these parts. In any case, the creature is the third wild animal I've seen in forty-eight hours, and I haven't said one word about the two randy iguanas racing along the seawall behind my father's building last week. "It's my mother again," I say to M, and just as I hear myself say those words, a blue jay squawks over our heads and we laugh at ourselves again.

The Freedom of Failure

2009 | A few months before her death, Denise and I develop a plan for her to see the new house in Springs. I want her to walk through the gardens, to stare down into the fish pond, to look at the spring light pooling in through the skylights. And maybe I think the visit would be a boon to her, to keep her going forward through rough times.

So, the train. Too many steps up and down into stations. Not enough bathrooms; she needs to be near a bathroom. The jitney isn't much better. Philadelphia to Amagansett: even in the best travel conditions we're talking five hours and that's not counting waiting time or layovers. We decide finally that she'll take the train from Philadelphia to Metropark. An hour ride. I'll meet her at Metropark and we'll drive over the Goethals Bridge, across Staten Island, over the Verrazano Bridge, the Belt Parkway, the Southern Parkway, the Sunrise Highway, the Montauk Highway, and take as much time as we want to get there. I'll map out possible stops along the way. For some reason, the thought of driving past the Parachute Ride and Deno's Wonder Wheel with her strikes me as especially appealing, though it will be unlikely she'll notice what I'm pointing out. She'll be talking fervently, with concentration on her face, looking a little above the brake lights of the car in front of us.

In the weeks ahead, we talk about the trip every few days, where Denise will sleep, what she might need to bring along. All the things she brought to the Pines and more. And every time I drive through the tunnel of trees toward our house, I imagine her making the small Denise sounds of approval.

2010 | One day, many months after her death, Denise's sister-in-law, Nancy, mentions reading an essay in which I make an appearance.

As soon as Nancy tells me about the essay, I tell her excitedly, oh, please, send it right now. I have not known this essay existed and I'm greedy to see it. I keep checking my inbox waiting for it to appear, and when it doesn't appear, I try to busy myself with a hundred other things. I cannot help but wonder if Nancy has reservations after her initial decision to tell me about the piece. Maybe she sees an aspect about the portrait of me that I might not find too sweet. The title, "The Freedom of Failure," certainly rivets my attention. If I make an appearance in it, then, well, maybe I'll learn about the tension between camaraderie and competition and how she saw those things playing out between us. At least I didn't imagine it, and on that level I feel an unexpected comfort. Every time I think of the essay, I feel my heart rate slow. The aperture of my attention widens.

And if I don't want to hear it? Shock is better than silence; shock makes us feel awake. What a thing, to be spoken to, anew, by someone whose voice you never thought you'd hear again, except for her walking toward you one day, in a dream.

Twenty-four hours pass and still no essay in my box. There are many ways to fend off disappointment, and I spend the day being more productive than usual: writing a long letter to a student, writing a blog post, writing emails to friends I haven't answered in a long time, boring business emails that require a certain amount of cheer I have to pull up from down in me. I don't even need my usual cup of coffee at five o'clock: look at my energy, concentration, my refusal to sit still for a single second. I chew the flavor out of all twelve sticks of cinnamon gum, and I'd probably start chewing some more if there were another pack within reach. I'd chew and chew until I spit it out in the trash, until the taste is pure chemical, until I'd never want another stick of gum again. And I wonder how many days I should wait before I say, hey, Nancy. Did you forget that essay?

2009 | M and I get in the car one day and set out for Camden, New Jersey. Camden would seem like an unlikely destination for a hot summer weekend in August, but it is the site of Walt Whitman's house, the only house he owned in his lifetime. We've been here before, thirteen years before, but we're coming back as M has been commissioned to write an article about the house, which would require a refreshed eye. Who knows? Maybe the house *has* changed in thirteen years. We drive down Martin Luther King Jr. Boulevard. We take in a grassy park, a marina, and an outdoor concert hall on the same spot from which Whitman took the ferry to Philadelphia. We see acres and acres of empty lots, simultaneously rural and desolate, as if an entire community had decided to pack up and go. But Whitman's house stands firm in gray-beige clapboard. And maybe that's why I'm not disappointed when we find out, by way of a sign, that the house is closed for vacation. "We should have called," we probably moan at once, and there's an almost comic acceptance to our predicament. This is what you get when you choose not to plan out the next hour ahead. On the steps next door sits a young man with a kind, curious face. We get to talking. He seems to know the house, love the house, and I like knowing that he knows that Bram Stoker and Oscar Wilde were visitors. He has watched the outsiders come to his neighborhood, he has met people who wouldn't have visited this block otherwise, and he has taken them in, thought about their funny shoes, considered the looks of awe and focus on their faces. Just as Whitman's book takes us all in, from the distance of a hundred years ago.

We turn down Haddon Avenue toward Harleigh Cemetery on the eastern edge of town. The grave would not be closed for vacation; graves are always open for business. At least on a hot Saturday in summer. But the grave is not so easy to find. Its location is eclipsed by signs marking the final resting place of another Camden poet, the haiku poet Nick Virgilio, who in his life must have made sure that visitors looking for Walt's grave would see his first. (In life, one of Nick's projects was the city's Walt Whitman Center, and after all that work in another poet's memory, who could not have been a little competitive?) Only after making a few wrong turns, past phragmites and a lake filled with blond water do we find the often-photographed mausoleum in a dense glen of ivy and trees. It might be tangential to mention that I was born in the hospital on the hill overlooking the grave, but it's true: a mere two hundred feet away. It makes me wonder whether my hospital room was pointed toward that grave, or at least turned in that direction. From birth to death—and my mother holds the moist infant me in her arms.

We park. We get out and slam the doors. We walk up to the gate to the Whitman family crypt, where Walt's mother, father, and brother lie stacked together inside the dank, moldy space, messy with spiderwebs. But if the whole family is side by side, then why is the name Walt Whitman etched into the arch above? A totalizing vision. He designed the building, after all; why not simply: Whitman? The two of us are confused by the hubris of it, and our discomfort is only heightened by the chiggers making a feast of our bare ankles. The smell of the Cooper River wafts over the weeds. Part pea soup, part rotting bone pulled up from a wetland, part sick. It is not a healthy-water smell. The smell sends us back to the car, where we roll up the windows, turn on the manufactured air full blast, and dedicate ourselves to scratching our bare arms and legs until they're speckled with little red dots.

We drive up Haddon Avenue past boarded-up blocks and clusters of men hanging outside the few storefronts we see. The day has been big. We've been shaken by what we've seen; we just can't put a name to that feeling yet. Should we need to? In truth, our hopes for this visit haven't actually panned out—we can already see that now. But that kind of vague disappointment seems to be true of all things we long for too much. There's a physical quality to the aftermath, like the letdown that comes after having eaten too much sugar.

I send an email to Denise once we're back in the hotel, across the Delaware in Philadelphia. It's not a long email—simply, *Hey, we're in your town. Yes, on the other side of the city. Philadelphia. Sorry*

I haven't given you more warning but it was a spontaneous trip. Are you up for brunch tomorrow? Someplace close to you? Someplace easy? We're only here for the day, but if it doesn't work out, I'll come down and see you very soon. I love you.

I don't hear from Denise until the next morning. I can feel the labor in her note: a mix of capital letters, lowercase letters, misspellings, and unnecessary spaces. I can feel the supreme concentration behind each word, the effort and failure to get each word right. I give her a call, the connection is bad—or maybe that's her voice. It's quieter, shakier, and more tenatative than I would have expected, but then again that is probably the cell phone connection.

"Are you sure you're up for this?" I say to her. "We don't have to. I know I should have called you before."

"No," she says. "We must. I'm fine." And we agreet to meet at Parc, her new favorite place, on Rittenhouse Square at eleven o'clock.

M and I are seated at a table in the raised section of the restaurant. We're trying to relax, we're tearing off too much bread from the basket on the table. We watch the waiters move across the black-and-white checked floor, smell the hard mineral smell of poached egg from someone else's plate. I tell M, *this isn't going to be easy. You haven't seen her in a long time.* And he assures me he'll be fine. He is used to illness. He does well, he says, in the company of those who are sick. Someone throws a Frisbee across the street, in the park, and a Bernese mountain dog jumps, lifts, catches the Frisbee in her mouth with a snap, and takes it away, head lowered, as if she's privy to a funny thing only she knows about. She lies down and gnaws on its red rim, lying in wait for other dogs to notice her good fortune.

And just then Denise's ex is standing at the table. I'm not sure he even says hello to us. He sits down with us, as if it would always be clear that he'd be joining us. I have no problem with him joining us; he's been so involved in Denise's day-to-day care; he's helped to find her a good living space and he's paying her rent. He tells us that the two of them meet at Parc every Sunday, just at this time. I try to push back the sensation that there's trouble in the air. Perhaps they have an announcement to make. Maybe they're getting married again after having lived apart so long. B has proposed getting married again to Denise as a way to make sure she'd have the best health insurance coverage, the best care. And though Denise was initially confused by this, maybe she has since settled into the idea.

But my questions are shut off once M's hand covers his mouth. Tears brim. A look of distress, genuine distress, creases his forehead. Denise is trying her best to creep out of the cab outside. B springs up from his seat. He walks out the front door to assist her, but where is the Denise I know? She isn't the Denise of months ago, with her vigor and sass, her determination to look fine, go forth, in spite of murderous treatments. Of course she's impeccably dressed: camouflage tank top, taupe scarf tied around her neck, lots of bare skin. The only concession to comfort is her sneakers, blocky white sneakers that must give her more traction than any other shoe. And there's her port, just above her collarbone, the bruised square of skin around it exposed for all to see. It is her bit of a fuck-you to a world that would like to say disease doesn't exist, disease happens to people I shouldn't have to see. She is still beautiful, but her particular kind of beautiful cannot conceal how much weight she's lost or the slowness of her walk. Each step takes such effort, and I can tell that the people near her are trying their best not to look. If we're lucky, one or two might know exactly what's going on, and they might be urging her forward, in silence. Or else they want her to go away. Maybe both.

And yet that smile on her face! A smile that could turn diamonds to black powder, which sounds more like her description than mine. The two of us sit side by side, B and M across the table, and the four of us do our best to demonstrate, through casual conversation, that disaster is not upon us. What do we talk about? The old points of reference don't matter so much these days, though Denise is still wondering how she's going to teach next month, and M is telling her, you don't want to teach, why would you want to teach? Just take the semester off and rejuvenate. Use that time to get massages and read novels, don't you think? And Denise slides over to another topic, not exactly ignoring the advice, but giving herself the freedom to bring up just what she wants to bring up. If illness doesn't give us freedom, then what does it give us? Maybe we're not talking so much about freedom, but her tact monitor. What could tact be when it takes so much to get from one second to the next? And whoever said that the mind must move in a straight line? One minute she's funny, one minute she's sarcastic. My God, her mind is all over the place. Each thought is another roll of the dice, and there's no better demonstration that human personality is as reliable as chemicals and chance. All of this happens with a big goofy grin on her face. It would be a mistake if I didn't say there wasn't some fun in all this—see me put my arm around her shoulder as B aims the camera at us again and again. Hear the popping sounds? And if she knew how much she was sounding like my mother, my dead mother—the abrupt shifts in tone, the jokes with no context—she would stop it right now. So this is what happens to all things, I think, as two girls in the tallest possible high heels clomp and laugh down the sidewalk, bare arm in bare arm.

2010 | The email from Nancy comes in late one evening amid a cluster of other emails. She apologizes for the misunderstanding. I don't appear in any essay—or she's never had a copy of such an essay. She doesn't even know if the piece even exists; it is likely yet another essay dreamed of, or in a half-finished state. But if there's no record of an essay, there's certainly an email about the essay, a letter she sends to me.

I read Denise's email once, stop, then read it all over again. It takes me a second to figure out that this is a tough-love letter to Nancy, a letter in response to some misunderstanding between

Nancy and Denise—or between Nancy and someone else in the family. The gist is this: since Denise has failed at everything, her work, her friendships, her relationships, she's grown up and Nancy should, too.

There were dozens of Denises—a Denise for this friend, a Denise for that friend. That could be said of all people who have a genius for friendship. But—I shake my head. The email is composed in a tone Denise wouldn't have wanted me to hear. It is a tone that identifies her role in her family, the expressive big sister who also happens to be the advice giver. It's not a side I'm eager to know right now. I want my Denise, selfishly. I want her to speak to me, only to me right now.

I come upon one passage in the email: *When Paul stopped talking to me, he was simply too busy for me. I could accept that. I didn't take it personally.*

My hands are flat against the laptop keys. For a second they look distant to me, like another person's hands, then they come in closer, clearer, and all I see are lines, bones, and veins, the fine light hairs curling over the knuckles.

Clearly this letter was written during the year and a half of our great distance.

Is that dust inside my nostrils, or is there an oil leak on the street nearby?

I stuff a wet bedspread into the clothes dryer. *Yes, you had nothing to do with it. Me. All me. Take no responsibility for anything.*

"And what about North Carolina?" I say aloud.

Then I stuff a second wet bedspread into the dryer. I press the button, taxing the efficient machine with too much sodden weight.

I walk back and forth around what little there is of the apartment. If I had a bigger place, I'd walk from room to room, looking for a dirty floor to clean. What am I feeling? If I were in the mood to be a proper patient I could say, interest, betrayal, annoyance, excitement. I could probably keep on filling the rest of this page, but words fail in the face of strong emotion. They hold too little; they don't pour into one another the way I want them to. There are solid walls between each word, and even if I named every abstraction, the list would never tell the complete story. There would always be another word to follow the last word.

I sit in the living room chair, looking at the jar that holds our late dog's ashes. An apartment full of urns: our dog's urn, our cat's urn, M's late lover's urn.

I stay up till one, two hours past my bedtime. I'm feeling, I tell myself, which is better than feeling nothing. To be pissed at the dead—this is where these days have taken me. For God's sake. It makes as much sense as being mad at the sidewalk, the cracks in the surface, the pieces of chewing gum blackened and crushed by so many feet. But I am not just mad, truly. It would be easier to sit with these feelings if I were simply mad.

A thought leans into me like a shoulder I can't see: my life would be larger if I could hold the dark side of Denise alongside the bright.

The Narrow Door

2009 | Another note comes in from Nancy. It is Wednesday, the middle of August. Denise has taken a turn, and she thinks I should come right away.

I look out at the Springs backyard, the late-sumer heap of vine, rose, bamboo, and leaf. The brevity of the note makes me sluggish. Philadelphia. I do not want to go to Philadelphia, especially at this point in the summer when so many people are traveling, irritable. Especially with it being—what, two trains away. Six long hours. I just want to be still. I just want to sit on the living room couch until Denise gets better again. She will get better again. And I am surprised that Nancy doesn't have the wherewithal to see that right now.

Maybe this is why Denise hasn't answered my emails since our visit last week.

I walk to the window again. The view outside the window grows smaller, the edges less distinct.

Denise will get better tomorrow. I know she'll get better.

An hour later I write to Nancy to tell her I will be leaving tomorrow on the 5:57 a.m. train.

I'm standing over Denise's bed, then sitting beside her. She doesn't look any different from how she looked at our brunch, but her eyes have been closed a full twenty-four hours, and she hasn't talked in that long. The speed with which I've gotten to the hospice is already a memory: Nancy picking me up at Thirtieth Street Station, elevator lifting to a high floor. Hugging Denise's mother, hugging Austen, hugging relatives, shaking hands. There is a surreal quality to the combination of orderliness and intensity in the air, the serene waiting room overlooking Center City, William Penn's statue atop

City Hall, the sleek modernism of the PSFS building. The sky over Center City looks troublesome, as if it's about to darken and break and express itself.

I am alone with my friend. I am surprised to be given this private time with her. There are at least a dozen relatives out in the waiting room, each of whom would like to do what I'm doing right now. Only yesterday she was awake and present, still telling the workers that the hospice stay was temporary, a place she'd be leaving after she felt better in a few days. That changed when Austen's best friend from New York arrived. She cried then as I'm told she cried when she heard I was coming. "Paul's coming?" she said, and her eyes went wide. As if a visit from me should be a surprise. Denise.

But I have come too late. She's not even the person I knew. I look at her sleeping face, grab her big warm toe poking out from beneath the sheet: monkey feet. It's not even Denise's face anymore: it's impersonal, a mask. She's breathing, head turned to the right, but her eyes are closed for good now. As awkward as it is to admit it, I'm relieved that we don't have to say the usual final things. Too much pressure, and how could human language ever carry us to whatever is coming next? Better to hold on to her toe. Better to think of peace. Better to wish her out and away, as her mind and body are already wanting two different things, and the fight isn't going to be pretty. But should I be surprised by that?

Then I change my mind. It is hard not to say all the deathbed things one has absorbed from books. It is hard to find the right phrase that might be carried off, beyond consciousness. She moistens her lips and coughs from deep in her throat. I sit down beside her and tell her I've been rereading her work all week. I tell her I've gone back to *Good Deeds*. I tell her I've read her essays, tell her about coming upon "Woman of Heart and Mind," her piece about motherhood and her brief relationship with Sam. I want her to hear what I'm saying. My feelings about her work should not be a surprise; she shouldn't have to be reassured just hours from the end. It's as if I'm still confronting the old accusation, at least implicitly: I don't love her work enough. Would it ever be possible to love her work enough? But I don't know what else to give her right now.

This room feels lonely. This room seems to need other people in it. I know there's a script, and even though I don't want the script, I feel as if I'm required to perform its parts.

I don't remember whether Denise's mother comes to get me at the door, or whether I've just decided to walk down the hall. In the waiting room, Nancy and Joey hand me a large envelope of Denise's work, and I read everything inside, from pieces she wrote as a teenager to newer stories, a few drafts short of finished. The lights are too bright for my eyes. I know the sky is glowering outside, but I do not raise my head to watch it change. I read and I read, as if reading is the only thing I can think of to keep me in the chair. On the other side of the room, Denise's family looks at the Food Channel with interest, where the baker in question prepares a cake with one too many layers of icing.

2010 | I'd already suspected the trip would be significant weeks before our departure, and now M and I are walking up the plank to the ferry. It would be impossible for the trip not to be significant, on an island we'd never been to, thirty miles out from the mainland. We're not here for a vacation, but for a reading we're giving together, and since the island is an effort to get to, we long ago decided to stay an extra day. It helps that Ned is much appreciated in Nantucket—no more agreeable creature to bring to Nantucket than a golden retriever. As it is, Ned is already exhausted from greeting even before he's trotted off the ferry. A handful of children surround him on the upper deck, rubbing him and playing tug-of-war with his chewy, while he rolls over on his back and shows everyone his belly, overstimulated by all those small hands in his fur.

Are we nervous? Of course we are. But the reading goes well. Our friends Joy, Maggie, Linda, and Laura are in the audience, happy to see us. We're happy to see them. And the landscape beyond town couldn't be darker, more mysterious. Moors, Japanese black pines, and other stunted vegetation. Part Scotland, part Florida Keys, part Pine Barrens of my youth. The landscape already feels like a representation of a mind-state, and I'm already looking forward to the day when I will come back, in less stressful moments.

The next morning, we take a dog walk high on a cliff along Nantucket Harbor with Len, one of the hosts of the reading, and his dog, Swearengen. The two dogs wrestle and rush, running in circles that get wider and wider. Ned is almost running at a forty-five-degree angle, mouth open, eyes wild, he's going that fast. At one point they are so close to the edge of the cliff that I tell them to stop, but they just keep on running. Ned slops into a mudpit. We are walking higher and higher into a heavy sky, too wintery for August. I am weighed down by three layers of clothes. Len points to a grassland and says, that might be the most endangered landscape in America. And they once wanted to build a Marriott here.

We head back to the car. The wet dogs soak their shapes into the upholstery.

Only an hour ago, at nine o'clock mass, the priest uttered these words as part of the intercessions, the only words I remember from those fifty minutes: *You lead us to salvation through the narrow door.*

2009 | We try very hard to keep busy in the overlit waiting room, though it is hard to keep busy when we haven't brought anything to occupy us. It would have seemed wrong to bring anything—a book, a notebook, a laptop—disrespectful to the dying. I suspect this waiting is killing us, but no one can admit to such a thing. And no one can go outside for a walk, for coffee or a sandwich, for who knows when we might be called in? The truth is we're lost without Denise. If she weren't down the hall, she'd have had an activity planned for us. She'd be telling stories, she'd be distracting us from all this death at hand. But all we have right now is time, achingly slow time, which has nothing to do with the time outside, where people rush to meetings, or drop off the kids at summer school. How many tasks does one not get done in a single day? That's how most of us live our lives, but that's not our problem right now. Denise's family and I are holding ourselves still in the room of light. We're waiting for the hand on the forearm, the shoulder, the hand that will bring us back to ourselves.

The hospice nurses seem to know this about us and they ask, kindly, but not too kindly, if they could bring us anything. Coffee? Water? A cup of tea?

Someone comes by and turns on the lamp.

2010 | At the motel in Nantucket, M talks of taking Ned for a walk into town. It is a long walk to town, a good mile along a busy road without a sidewalk. I'm not so sure any puppy could be strong enough to walk a mile and back, and I say it. I have to say it.

"Ned will be fine," he says, leaning over, tying his sneaker.

I look over at Ned, who's already excited by the jingle bell sound of his leash. A humid wind pours through the slats of the jalousies. "Are you sure? Puppies need sleep. It doesn't make sense," I say, and rub my arms from the cold.

The truth is, nothing makes sense these days. No emotional logic, no context, no explanation for fiery moods. More and more M is as touchy as Denise, at least the Denise I remember from that night in North Carolina.

"Sense?" he says. *Sense?* And looks at me as I've said the foulest word in the notebook. He leaves the room, biting into his lip. Ned follows behind him, jumping and leaping.

I do not move from my place on the bed. It doesn't help matters that the night before, a blogger has decided to praise a story of mine on his blog. The same blogger has said harsh things about M's work in the past. I'm not so naive as to think that the blogger doesn't have subterranean motivations, but that doesn't stop me from posting a link to his good review on *my* blog. I feel crummy about this. I feel as if I've chosen my own work over my loyalty to M's work, and it just doesn't taste good. It tastes worse—I feel it souring my stomach—with each passing hour. Should I take it down? I truly consider this. Even if I did take it down, I'm not sure that would stop the agitated feelings between us now.

I stand at the window. The sky is so much darker than it should be at four in the afternoon. Maybe Len was right about the three inches of rain in the forecast. On the parking lot, two boys play catch with their father. They throw the softball with a steadiness and freneticism that suggest they're going to be inside for a long time. They know more about the weather than I do, so I turn on the forecast.

Beyond the parking lot, the phragmites rattle as the wind pushes them back and forth. It's the sound of my childhood summers. A little anxious, vaguely tropical, the wind pushing weeds as a storm came up. Wavelets slapping the bulkhead along the lagoon, the docks. Blue sky, charcoal sky, and wigeons and buffleheads flying off in all directions, looking for a place to take cover.

An hour later M walks back through the door with Ned. His mood is not better. If anything, it is worse. He has thought about sense. Sense, he says, stands in the way of so much. Sense stands in the way of spontaneity, expression. Sense stands in the way of risk. Since when have I become the avatar of sense? I never expected to be taken literally; I was only concerned about Ned, who admittedly looks just fine as he pushes his black nose into my leg. But this fight is about a problem I can't put my finger on. It goes on and goes on. It shakes the rafters of the room, though neither of us is yelling. The people in the next room are laughing—or is that a show on TV? "I can't go on like this" meets "That's it, it's over." And I say the latter. I think this means I've done the nasty deed I've been expected to execute all along. I am astonished I could say such a thing. Could I imagine having said such a thing two months ago? Well, no. I was so innocent then, though I thought I'd seen everything. I can hardly lift myself from the bed, and we promised to go to a dinner party in less than a half hour.

There are tears shed. "I don't think I can go," M says.

"We have to go," I say, standing up. I wipe my nose on the back of my fist. "You'll feel a lot better."

I'm not even sure why I say this. There would be no harm in saying that one or both of us just fell ill. That wouldn't be lying. At this moment we are both ill, even if our illness can't be pinned down to a fever or sore throats.

And somehow we manage to dry our eyes and say hello to Joy, who's walking toward us, grinning her big grin, by the motel pool. And somehow we manage to be pleasant dinner companions at the dinner party in the big house on the beach. I sit next to Joy at dinner, and aside from talking about dogs and other animals, we talk about books. I ask her questions about her stories, about her use of imagery and plot. I take a sip from my wine and then another. I am enthralled, so happy. To sit beside my favorite writer: how can my happiest night also be my saddest? I look over at M, who's talking to Seward, across the table. More red wine is poured. I wonder if anyone else can tell what's going on between us. Maybe. Joyce, Seward's wife, wonders why everyone is laughing when no one at the table really knows the others that well. She says she feels separate from it, talks of hearing that laughter a few minutes back from the kitchen. We are uncomfortable to hear her interpretation, though the exchange it triggers entrances us. We all admit that laughter has very little to do with happiness. It is about release. Nervousness about the trap of composure. Then conversation of any sort is difficult for some minutes. We step outside to the porch. Spotlights shine on a dinghy hitched up in the beach grass. And just before we head back inside, the ferry glides into the harbor, deadly silent. The harbor is black. What is it about a lit boat headed toward shore at night? one of us asks. It's like a scene from *Amarcord,* Joy says. An unexpected gust of wind shivers the beach grass. I smell rain, fresh rain, on the air. It's getting ready to pour. I can already imagine it pounding the dunes. And we wonder about the people in the boat, if they're looking forward to seeing who's meeting them at the dock.

2010 | To think you can love someone so well that he'd forget the dead, forget his pain. To think of love as a laser beam of attention. To think you could beam that attention toward him in such a way that he wouldn't even know you were doing it. To learn that your attention is doomed. Unwelcome, better having been put to other uses: helping the poor, working for the environment, for animals. To learn that you are only a pale winter sun, when you once thought you could have made the hillsides green.

2009 | Everyone who's here for Denise is gathered inside this little room, little oven. There must be a dozen of us. Now we have a job to do, now we're helping to write the old story: she died surrounded by family and friends. Austen closest to her mother's face, hand on her brow; Denise's mother on the other side. Her ex-husband beside Austen, me by her feet. All the lights and lamps are off. Flames shudder in the votives. Joni sings from Joey's laptop, the bare-bones demo of "Good Friends," from the CD I made for her many months back. No one in the room knows that Denise once called it our song when it first came out in 1985, and the timing of it feels as if we're passing a secret back and forth. In a minute, Joni's cover of "It's All Over Now, Baby Blue" comes on. And this is the moment where Denise would guffaw. Talk about timing. Irreverent Denise: no narratives of grace and consolation for her.

We're watching her face. It's a little like waiting for a movie to start, and it's unbearable, this watching, this waiting. What group of human beings could ever be in practice for such a thing? We probably realize this, in our separate ways, at about the same time. Along with the shock that we wish the movie would get to the heartbreaking part. This is time without boundaries. Time without boundaries is a little like, well—we're in a boat, think of that, a little rocking boat, a hundred miles out, no trees or shorelines in sight. But we don't want to hurry this on either. We want Denise to be aware of us in her bones and blood. This is why we're here. We're all, in a sense, going out with her.

A nurse comes in. The nurses, the calming presence of the nurses. Their neutrality, never too concerned, never too near. I can't imagine what it might be like to be them, to live inside such intensity day after day. Are they clear-glass houses? Or do they shut all their doors and windows once they're off duty? I don't know how else they could buy food, pay bills, wait to be called at the DMV without thinking of the ways, all the ludicrous ways, we go about distancing ourselves from the fact that we're all on the way to dying. Maybe they are simply in better practice than we are. Maybe it isn't too hard to get where they are. You get a summons for jury duty on the day of a best friend's graduation: so what? You think of that beautiful writer down the hall, the one who made you laugh as you slid that gigantic needle into her arm, and you think, well, if she could do *that* . . .

The room gets warmer. It is six o'clock. The storm that has been building all day is finally letting loose. Thunder rolls through the city, lightning flashing against the walls, but there's a kindness about the storm sounds. A bit of comedy, too. "She's not going out easy," an uncle says. "Just listen to that." And some of us laugh, a relief to laugh in the middle of such intensity.

Waiting. Is Denise aware that we're waiting? It must be hard enough to die, to slip out of your body without worrying about the people you're leaving behind. There is a story of a man out on Long Island, a former neighbor. He found a good woods, mashed down the weeds the way a deer would, then lay down and went to sleep on the ground. He covered himself with leaves. The story is passed around as neighborhood legend: the saddest story in the world. Such a gentle man. Meticulous gardener, good friend, frozen in snow for days on end, and this is how creation watches out for him? Yet it doesn't sound so bad to me. Would I want so many faces, even if they are loving faces, trained on me when it's my time to go? No, not me.

I hold on to her toe a little while longer. It is still warm. An hour goes by, then is it two? The thunderstorm outside the window has passed. Then one by one we decide we've had enough. Some of us wander to the waiting room. Some of us wander off toward the elevator, heads down, as if we've disappointed someone, though we don't exactly know who that someone is.

Denise's closest family members stay by her side through the night. She dies at some point close to 6 a.m.

The elevator is falling. I'm remembering my friend. It would make sense that someone so attached to her writing—the allure of the perfect shape, which must always be rejected—would want to mess things up a little at the end.

2010 | We walk home with Joy through the dark. The rains and winds lash the trees; we need to shout to be heard over them. A car flies by, flings water in a wide, flamboyant arc. The road goes dark again after its headlights disappear around the bend. We're stepping through cold puddles that we can't see, deep ruts in the sandy road. The air smells of crawl space. I let M, Joy, and Ned walk ahead. I hang back a little, if only because I don't want them to see how much I don't like rain in my eyes, or on the top of my head. The sole is already pulling away from my shoe.

Joy gives each of us a hug as we say good night at the motel. "Good night, guy," she says to me. "Good night," we call back. Joy backs her jeep, with top down, out of the parking space. We walk back to our room wet, completely wet. We peel off our clothes, drop them in piles at the foot of the bed. Ned's tail is wagging. Who sleeps where? I don't know where, but maybe that's why the fighting starts up again. It's hotter this time, accustations cooked through dinner. They are the saddest sentences ever spoken. Well, of course that's not true. Sadder words are spoken all the time, in the house across the street, in the planes above our heads. People go on. But that doesn't make it any easier for Ned. He's up on the bed, on which he tears up his blue water dish into shreds, not with his usual vigor or joy but with frustration. He's feeling what we're feeling and he doesn't know where to put any of it.

I decide to sleep on the love seat instead of my usual left side of the bed. The love seat is torn, plaid, infested with fleas—at least two feet shorter than the length of my body, but that's where I'd rather spend the night. I curl up on my side, closing my eyes against the porch light coming in through the window, yellow light, which we used to call "bug light" when I was a kid. And the rain, which is noisy in its force, turning all surfaces—air conditioners, car hoods, pavements—into drum kits.

"You don't have to sleep there," M says, calmer now, from a few feet away on the bed.

"I'll be all right," I say.

A car door slams in the parking lot. It opens up, then slams again, with more emphasis.

"I don't think you know how to break up," M says, quieter now, after a silence. "It doesn't have to be like high school. Fifteen years does not end in one night."

I let myself sink into that thought. I'm scratching into my forearms and ankles. I smell the faintest hint of blood beneath my nails. And a man and a dog fall asleep without another sound as it rains and rains and rains.

Anne Carson: "It is stunning, it is a moment like no other, / when one's lover comes in and says I do not love you anymore."

2009 | Nancy writes to ask if I will deliver the eulogy. I don't hesitate to say yes. Of course I'll speak for Denise. But words—what words could I say to make Denise, all the Denises, real to those people in the church? And how to speak of her in church when she'd already told me she'd stopped believing in God? What she believed in were stories, stories in which the cruelest things happened between people. In her last months, she couldn't stop talking about the stories of A. M. Homes, in which the parents smoke crack and a teenage girl attacks a Barbie doll with a razor blade, and good deeds are never rewarded.

Maybe she saw those plotlines as figures for what cancer does to the body. I never got to ask.

2010 | I awake the next morning to the terrible sound of a dog wailing in the parking lot. The door opens, the rain is sheeting, and M is at the door with Ned. It is Ned crying, Ned who had sat down upon a hill of ants, flushed out of their colony by the downpour. M puts Ned on the bed—yes, I have made my way to the bed by now—and the three of us are in it together for the first time since the previous night. My hand is on Ned, whose short wet fur I'm stroking. He stops yipping in a bit, and in a little while, he's back to himself again, head down between two paws. He looks toward the headboard as if he's thinking. When I stop stroking, I put down my hand, palm up. I smell like dog. M reaches for my hand, holds it. I try to hold it back, but I can't give over my full grip to him. No, I'm doing the best I can. I'm crying soundlessly. My feelings are too dire for hysterics, then M cries soundlessly, too. He walks into the bathroom, blows his nose into a piece of torn-off toilet paper. Ned looks at me as if he senses we're about to move again. He starts panting, standing up, the sand falling off his coat, onto the bedspread, the pillows. Then I'm standing up, walking about the room. I turn on the TV news, I'm opening drawers, doing what I can to clean up for the housekeeper. In an hour we have a ferry to catch, and the wind will just not stop.

2009 | Bags in hand, M and I are walking along the Montauk Highway to the jitney stop in Amagansett. Funeral at nine tomorrow; we're leaving for Philadelphia the night before. Thick trees, trimmed limbs, waxy glowing shrubs: it is the kind of world where you might think nothing brutal could ever happen. The grass blues in the twilight, the sprinkler hoses seep. Tiny flies go round and round beneath the eaves. Then just past the farm market, a young guy yells out the open window of his pickup: *Hey fags*, with the biggest smile. It is more brutal for the smile attached to these words, but I simply lift my hand in greeting. Let him think it's a wave. He wants us to be pierced. He wants us to remember this night as violent, sadistic, but he will not get that satisfaction from me.

"Nice," says M to the back of the truck, which is already ahead of us, on the edge of town.

I really don't feel it: what that fuckhead tries to do to us.

2010 | The fast-ferry waiting room is packed. As we are in New England, and not just any New England but Nantucket, people are cheerful, distant, cool, controlled. At least people are trying to be those things, which might account for the fogged-up windows. The nervous breaths exhaled but hidden from sound and view. We've already heard that the slow ferry has been canceled due to wind; all flights from the island also canceled. But the workers at the desk say the 10:35 is still on schedule. I sit on the edge of a bench, pretending to give my complete attention to the messages on my phone, while M sits down the aisle from me, Ned curled up beneath his chair.

A woman announces that the fast ferries are being canceled for the day, and the whole crowd rises, at once, without a huff or complaint. M and I stare straight ahead, too tired to be distraught. If this were an Ingmar Bergman film, which would it be—*Cries and Whispers, Scenes from a Marriage, Persona*? I play this game in my head, while the rain comes down harder outside the window. Everyone seems to have a place to go to: a house, a relative, a friend. I need to be by myself. If there were ever a day for lying in bed, this would be the kind of day for it.

M makes a call. Help comes in the form of Amy, one of our

hosts at the reading the other night. Amy has had a conversation with Maggie Conroy, the wife of Frank, my late teacher. M, Ned, and I will be staying at Maggie's for the day and night, which sounds like a wonderful thing—but to be civil in front of others again! To perform as if we haven't just hefted our weapons through battlefields. Haven't we already given enough blood? Apparently not, think the powers that be. They want us to go out on the field just one more time, just to make sure we're not going to draw guns or knives or swords. I am not yet ready to be a man of peace.

Minutes later, we are on the east side of Nantucket, off Polpis Road, where Maggie welcomes us at the front door of a contemporary house with sloping roof. It looks like the kind of house that might have wandered over the Sound from upstate Vermont—say the Goddard campus or a very pleasant commune. Vaulted ceiling, floorboards and beams retrieved from a tobacco barn in Pennsylvania. A pleasant smell, a little tea, wet raincoat, moist dog. I am not quite present to myself, and believe I am all the worst things: inward, distracted, exhausted, incapable of complete sentences without stops. Plus, I am wearing the same wet clothes I've been wearing for the past three days. The houseguest you've always dreamed of. But Ned and Neville, Maggie's ten-month-old puppy, are already going at it on the Oriental rug beneath the grand piano. They're doing what they can to distract us. Lunges and leaps, watching games. It is hard not to keep focused on the two dogs to see who might be the winner.

2009 | I don't know any other way to start. Cause and effect, verbs, action—all of that seems completely foreign to me right now. Shapely paragraphs, consoling thoughts—no. None of that belongs in this space. But I don't want to be all over the place. I'm not even sure the eulogy is about Denise, though I'm talking about her capacity for joy, the apotheosis of her work. Allan, the wounded son in *Good Deeds*, dancing with his sister in the final scene, singing "Sympathy for the Devil." Irv, their father, walking into the room, flapping the sleeves of his kimono. "What the hell?" in a voice three-quarters exasperation, one-quarter affection. But his son and his daughter ask him to join their dance, in spite of their mother's death, and all the pain in the household. Joy is what we want to inhabit after so much pain.

Her eyes: playful, wry, soulful.

Her charisma, her wattage. A movie star.

Her old plea, the old accusation: "Nobody loves me." Or worse: "You don't love me." And her joy when I shut my eyes, or gave her that look that said, I've had all I can take of you.

Her quickness to laugh, the laugh that came from deep in the body. Part silly, part womanly.

Her cup of scalding hot coffee, held with both hands, close to the collarbone and throat, even if it was ninety-seven degrees outside.

Her toned olive arms.

Her monkey feet.

Her ability to walk into any room and warm the atmosphere. A ray of energy moving right into you . . .

I'm getting through the eulogy. It's embarrassing to admit it; I like being up there with the priest, the cantor, the Eucharistic ministers. I like the height of the ceiling, the depth of the building, the quiet of the people in the pews. Their attention toward the front of things. I know how to speak in front of a congregation, and I'm practically listening to myself form the words. I am just a conduit. I'm wondering where that calm voice is coming from until I look out and see Mary, Denise's younger sister. I am talking about that night of the election, Denise getting up from the table to dance. I don't know why, of all moments, my eyes drift to Mary, but then I do. We understand—there's no other way to put it. It's an awareness of how long we've been known to each other through Denise as much as it is about Denise. And I don't break down—that's the last thing I want to do right now. I don't want the delivery to be about me. I breathe and I pause. I let my eyes drift down and my brain go blank. I slip down through the surface of a tank, fall, arms raised, all the way to the bottom. Then breathe and go on with the rest of the words.

It's not till I leave the church, walking down the aisle after the priest and family that I lose my composure, at least in my face. I can't keep holding it anymore, but I am trying not to make a scene of it. Maybe it's seeing so many people who were once in my life in those pews. They're back again, my old professors, grayer, more fragile versions of what they once were.

2010 | We watch the dogs tangle and roll and pull. We cry Stop! when they get too rough. The wind sleeks through the cracks in the house, the rain soaks the wood. There is a mellow sweetness inside, made sweeter by the lamps on in the middle of the day, the presence of Frank's grand piano in the center of the living room, the view through the window of the harbor, where the boats pull at their moorings. I wonder when the piano had last been played. If I were feeling better, I might go over and play a chord or two, but instead I imagine the ghost notes filling the barn-like space. Happy house, a summer night, Frank playing Charlie Mingus's "Goodbye Pork Pie Hat" to a room full of close friends, with drinks in hand, who nod, lean into the sound of his playing.

M and I drive to Sconset. We drive to Tom Nevers, where cars snake down the beach road for a demolition derby. It is still pouring, three-layer weather, but it is no longer the kind of rain that one can't spend some time in. Later Joy comes over for dinner, and she makes two martinis for me, and my neck, shoulders, and lower back relax. The light in the room gets softer. The voices get slower. We talk and laugh and play with the dogs. We talk a little bit more about animals and politics and books until Joy says good night, and in a while the two of us walk upstairs to our bedrooms. It is a relief that M and I are given separate bedrooms with single beds, on opposite ends of a hall. For a while we are not two people who have shared the same bed for almost sixteen years, but two brothers staying in our favorite sister's house. And in that way I don't have to think about him at all. Should the house fall in, he will be there. Should he miss one of the steps, I will be there.

Then he sticks his head in the room for a moment. "Sleep tight," he says with a smile. And is gone down the hall to his room.

If this house were a person, it would be a mother. The mother is forgiveness. The mother rocks peaceably in the wind, but stands up to the wind, too, even when a huge branch falls down on the roof. The wind is no match for the mother. Why mother? Maybe it is Maggie, who seems happy to have us around. Maybe it is the great open space of the house, which might also be a ship, the mother ship taking the passengers back and forth across the cold, clear Sound. Maybe it is the accumulation of all the people who have passed through this space, leaving their gladness behind. The house could almost convince you that there was never an ugly moment inside it. But we can guess that fights have happened here, certain words darker than they were ever meant to be. That is the story of any house, though we'd rather think otherwise. See that bright window across the street? Someone is leaning on the edge of the kitchen counter with both hands, looking away from the person he thinks he hates right now, that hate so close to love he can't even tell them apart.

The next morning the trees in Maggie's yard are almost still. A rush of wind pushes off some leaves and then it's still again. I stay in bed as long as I can, reading Frank's *Time and Tide,* flipping back to the map of Nantucket inside, before I sense it would be impolite to hang back any longer.

Downstairs M and Maggie are laughing as if there has never been anything but light in the world.

Then Neville leaps onto the bed and climbs onto me, barely disturbing me. How could a dog be so light and have such presence, such solidity? Actuality? He pulls himself up over to me, looks at me with an expression that says: *I'm glad you're in the house. You're going to be all right.* There is nothing inflated about the moment, nothing visionary. It's even funny. Neville is the Frank I remember from the workshop table, exactly twenty years ago. And just as that thought passes through my head, Neville jumps off the bed, walks down the hall without ceremony. He goes down to do what dogs do, nails clicking down the open planks of the staircase.

In the hour before the ferry leaves the three of us take a dog walk along the harbor. Ned and Neville have calmed down considerably. They're actually running, racing up and down the beach stairs of a cedar-shake compound atop an eroding dune. They repeat this process several times. We make jokes about the dogs alerting private security forces. We talk of soldiers cocking their guns, shooting the dogs quickly and efficiently as if they're rabbits. Earlier M had said that Ned looked sad that he'd never get along with Neville, but he'd take that back now. Their steps are already in sync.

I think: if I can know M after those words of last night, then maybe I will have passed through the narrow door.

I think: sunlight might be on the other side of that narrow door, but I have no clue as to what that sunlight might be.

Pasture of Darkness

2009 | The sky over the beach is part golden, part gray-blue cloud. There has never been a sky like it. It's a sky that doesn't know what weather it wants to be. Out to sea there must be a storm: foam rises higher and higher on the strand. The water is warm, tropical, which can happen when you're this far out on Long Island, where the Gulf Stream passes just miles off the coast. At Shinnecock Bay, forty miles to the west, that warm water passes through the narrow channel of the inlet, filling the bay with species you'd never otherwise find this far north. Lionfish, triggerfish, all the fish you'd expect in Florida. Then the bay temperature starts dropping on the first cold night in September. Do they go back out the channel, heading back to the waters that brought them here? Probably the river only takes them one way, and maybe they've always known that. But the crazy adventure that brought them here! The rushing current, the sun rising, the ring of fire at sunset. They look for a place to be still. They store up on plankton, algae, mollusks. They find a nook inside some favorite rocks and pilings and breathe and concentrate and bear into the cold.

We are worn out after the long ride back from Philadelphia. Before we go to bed that night—it is an early bedtime, ten o'clock?— we walk the beach at Indian Wells. People are building bonfires, gathering driftwood to burn. Blankets are anchored with stones and clam shells at the corners. A beach wagon is stuck in the sand. The sea is unexpectedly rough, waves breaking in double rows, one at the sandbar, the other a hundred feet out. Torches are lit. Could any night be more beautiful? A wave crashes onto my shorts, but I'm okay with it. Down the beach, a wave crashes all the way up to the dune line, swamping two women and their German shepherd, and they're okay with it, too.

2010 | Quarter to six in the evening. M speeds south on I-95 in Groton, Connecticut, as it now looks possible to make the six o'clock boat back to Orient Point, on Long Island's North Fork. A car idles in front of us in the exit lane, on the wide bridge over the Thames. A few turns to the left, a red light, maybe two, and M rushes up to the ferry booth. I have a reservation, he says. The man taps some figures into a keyboard. "You're on," says the ferry man. M drives, swerves, pulls ahead to lane three, and not two seconds after he stops, I get out of the car. All the other cars are already parked, brakes engaged. People chatter on the decks above, taking pictures, tempting gulls. They're looking toward the naval base for submarines, periscopes. I take my bags from the backseat and place them on the pavement. I hold Ned's head to my chest, breathe in the scent of his fur, still pungent, weedy from the beach. I say good-bye to M. I hug him longer than I would have expected to hug him, before I hurry across the tracks to the train station.

They are going to Springs, I am going to Manhattan. If all goes well, I should be in the apartment by ten thirty tonight.

The terminal is strangely underpopulated for a summer night. A boy and a girl run around in circles. Their shoes attack the floor, their voices booming up into the vaulted ceiling.

I stand at the windows, waiting for the white ferry to move past.

Does he wave at me? I am looking. M does wave back at me, from the deck of the second level.

A passing thought occurs to me: maybe the real love story of M and Paul might only be just beginning.

2009 | Denise's memorial reading takes place in November, down a dark hallway at City College. The event happens through the kind attention of a professor who offered us the space after coming across pictures of Denise I'd posted online. I never expected more than a classroom, but the college has even paid for food. Who will come to eat this beautiful food? I'm grateful, but also anxious that no one will show up—or worse, just a few. I want this to go well. No one comes to readings anymore, not even for famous writers, not in Manhattan. We're not even in the most accessible part of Manhattan, all the way up on 138th Street, blocks from the subway. First two undergraduates step at the door. They look inside. They look cautious, shy. I say hello—their careful gestures make me feel shy. They sit feet from the door, maybe because they're worried that the night might be too reverent, too tearful, too insidery. Then comes Denise's mother, then Austen and her fiancé, then a few of Denise's friends from way back. Iris's assistant editor, David, walks into the room along with my high school friend, Janet, a therapist, whom I haven't seen in years. My friends Susan and Sarah, excellent writers. I'm happy to see everyone. In a little while thirty-five people sit around a seminar table, facing a podium, waiting for a reading to begin.

M reads, Victoria reads, David reads, Joe reads, B reads. No one talks about Denise. No one is talking about missing her or the books that won't be written and read. We're listening to what we have. Six of us read from thirty years of work: novels, essays, stories. Patterns emerge. Variations in tone. The comic Denise against the serious Denise. In one story, the two sides in the same voice. What is it like to know a single human in time? That is the question that inevitably organizes our listening. There's nothing more absorbing than thinking about all these changes over the years. It's not that the progression is linear. It's just that her obsessions—the twin poles of shame and grace—move like a spiral, rotating around a core.

The program ends after eighty minutes, not a minute more. No one takes up too much time and space. There was never a ceremony that went off with so little work. We all say good-bye to one another, reluctant to step into the hall. We don't want this night to end. So a few of us linger, as a man, a complete stranger in the room, fills his pockets with bread.

I pull some grapes from a stem.

Then we turn off the lights.

2010 | One of Denise's old friends wants to let me in on a secret. In the past weeks Denise's friends have been calling to tell me Denise's secrets: men she slept with, men who came back to say good-bye— one to simply hold her through the length of an afternoon—after she'd told them she was dying. These friends have the honor of holding on to this piece of her. They're betraying Denise—they know that—but opening up our sense of her. What good is a secret if it cannot be betrayed? By telling me these secrets, they are making her come to life again, in them, in us. They are expecting secrets back—or an intimacy. She flickers for a bit before she's gone, just as most of them flicker and burn out over the months.

Another friend writes to tell me she has Denise's diary for the year 2004. She would like me to have it—but she would like to sit down with me first, in person, to interpret what is on the page. 2004—the year we didn't talk. I clench up inside—no, it isn't right! That year must stay cloistered. I want to keep asking questions, I want to believe that she's impossible to know, as all of us are impossible to know. How else to keep her alive in me? I want Denise to keep growing taller, wider: a redwood with many rings.

I am not yet ready to share her with anyone, not now.

The email goes unanswered.

2012 | How tempting it is to do the alchemical now. To turn darkness into light, bread into flesh, tin into gold, wine into blood. It's what narrative wants of us, at least this part of the narrative. It wants to comfort, not that we should necessarily link comfort to weakness. Couldn't there be some rigor to comfort? I'd like to think story could give it that, to give the hurting in us strength and power. So we will not leave the page without reserving a pasture for darkness, inscrutability. If we don't acknowledge that pasture, if we don't respect the secret creatures that might be grazing there, those creatures may turn on us. They might loom and howl and bear down on us because they need to eat, as all creatures need to eat. "One creature eats another," says Marie after Inan asks why some people love meat. "That's just the way of things." Marie doesn't say it with sorrow. She doesn't say it with anger. The world is not ugly to her. She says it as fact. But I don't want to eat the living—not Denise, not M, not the animals in the pasture or the trees. "You don't have to," says Marie. "That's the news. Here, have a glass of water. Drink." But there's no getting around the structure of the world. The world eats all things, and in doing that, the grass is fed. "The unkempt hair of graves," as Whitman describes grass. I step out with the others, onto the meadow, into the fragrant pond. I don't yet know what to make of any of this. And the creatures nestle beneath the trees before they start their eating again.

Acknowledgments

Love and thanks to Karen Bender, Deborah Lott, Elizabeth McCracken, Susan Stinson, and Lisa Zeidner for their friendship and for being such dedicated readers of this manuscript.

Love and thanks, too, to Polly Burnell, Maggie Conroy, Kathleen Graber, Lauren Grodstein, James Allen Hall, Marie Howe, Richard McCann, Angelo Nikolopoulos, Victoria Redel, Martha Rhodes, Katrina Roberts, Patrick Rosal, Salvatore Scibona, Oren Sherman, Lyrae Van Clief-Stefanon, Dawn Walsh, and Dara Wier. Also to my family: my father, Bobby, Michael, Sandy, Jordan. Carlos Castellar.

To the Piccoli family: love. To Austen.

Thanks to the Returning Residency program of the Fine Arts Work Center in Provincetown, where parts of this book were written. To Allison Devers and David Selden for the year in Asbury Park.

To Fiona McCrae, Katie Dublinski, Steve Woodward: the very best.

Michael Taeckens!

Emily Louise Smith. Stephanie Manuzak.

To J. S.

And to M. Of course.

PAUL LISICKY is the author of *Lawnboy, Famous Builder, The Burning House,* and *Unbuilt Projects.* His work has appeared in *Tin House, Fence, Ploughshares,* the *Iowa Review, Conjunctions,* and the *Offing,* among other magazines and anthologies. He is a graduate of the Iowa Writers' Workshop, and his awards include fellowships from the National Endowment for the Arts, the James Michener/Copernicus Society, and the Fine Arts Work Center in Provincetown, where he was twice a fellow. He has taught in the writing programs at Cornell University, New York University, Rutgers University–Newark, Sarah Lawrence College, the University of North Carolina Wilmington, and elsewhere. He currently teaches in the MFA Program at Rutgers University–Camden. He divides his time between New York City and Philadelphia.

The text of *The Narrow Door* is set in Warnock Pro. Book design by Connie Kuhnz. Composition by Bookmobile Design & Digital Publisher Services, Minneapolis, Minnesota. Manufactured by Versa Press on acid-free, 30 percent postconsumer wastepaper.